SPORTS STARS WITH HEART

Tim Duncan

CHAMPION ON AND OFF THE COURT

by J Chris Roselius

Enslow Publishers, Inc.
40 Industrial Road
Box 398
Berkeley Heights, NJ 07922
USA
http://www.enslow.com

Library of Congress Cataloging-in-Publication Data
Roselius, J. Chris.
  Tim Duncan : champion on and off the court / J. Chris Roselius. — 1st ed.
      p. cm. — (Sports stars with heart)
  Includes bibliographical references and index.
  ISBN 0-7660-2821-6
  1. Duncan, Tim, 1976—Juvenile literature. 2. Basketball players—United
States—Biography. I. Title. II. Series.
    GV884.D86R67 2006
    796.323092—dc22
    [B]   2006012544

Credits
Editorial Direction: Red Line Editorial, Inc. (Bob Temple)
Editor: Sue Green
Designer: Lindaanne Donohoe

Printed in the United States of America

0 9 8 7 6 5 4 3 2 1

To Our Readers: We have done our best to make sure all Internet addresses in this book were active and appropriate when we went to press. However, the author and the publisher have no control over and assume no liability for the material available on those Internet sites or on other Web sites they may link to. Any comments or suggestions can be sent by e-mail to comments@enslow.com or to the address on the back cover.

Photographs © 2006: AP Photo/Chuck Burton: 39, 47; AP Photo/Michael Conroy: 109; AP Photo/Eric Gay: cover, 1, 3, 11, 58, 76, 96, 101; AP Photo/ Karl DeBlaker: 29; AP Photo/Kevork Djansezian: 93; AP Photo/Ron Frehm: 68; AP Photo/Steve Helber: 23; AP Photo/Bob Jordan: 45; AP Photo/Andres Leighton: 80; AP Photo/Mark Lennihan: 64; AP Photo/Delcia Lopez: 85; AP Photo/Nick Procaylo: 55; AP Photo/Jeff Roberson: 105; AP Photo/ Tim Sharp: 21; AP Photo/Nick Wass: 35; AP Photo/Kathy Willens: 4; AP Photo/David Zalubowski: 3, 51

Cover Photo: San Antonio Spurs forward Tim Duncan scores against the
Los Angeles Clippers during a game December 13, 2005, in San Antonio.

CONTENTS

Duncan and Kenyon Martin vie for the ball during the 2003 Finals.

CHAPTER ONE

A True Leader

Playing in the NBA Finals was nothing new to Tim Duncan. But the 2003 Finals would be different. Without question, Duncan was the leader of the San Antonio Spurs, and there was no better time to display that than in Game 6 against the New Jersey Nets. It was a game that could clinch the NBA title for the Spurs, but they were struggling midway through the third quarter.

In front of a silent home crowd, San Antonio was trailing by ten points and was about eighteen minutes from being forced to play a Game 7. It was time for Duncan to step forward. It was time for him to come to the rescue.

Though standing almost seven feet tall, Duncan can just as easily hit a jump shot as he can dunk the ball. Needing a spark, Duncan showed off his shooting touch by lofting a high-arching shot over the hands of a Nets defender and swishing a jumper from eighteen feet. After grabbing a couple of rebounds on the defensive end, Duncan made a short jumper to cut New Jersey's lead to six, 59–53, with 3:19 remaining in the third quarter.

Duncan, however, is by no means a one-dimensional player. He is just as good passing the ball as he is shooting. New Jersey became determined to stop Duncan from scoring, double- and triple-teaming him whenever possible in the final quarter.

That still didn't stop Duncan as he twice passed out of those double-teams to spark a 19–0 run in the fourth quarter. With 6:33 remaining in the game, Duncan spotted an open Stephen Jackson and quickly passed the ball to him for a three-pointer and a 73–72 lead.

Nearly two minutes later, Duncan again found himself surrounded by Nets defenders. Out of the corner of his eye, he found Jackson setting up for a three-pointer. Without hesitation, Duncan whipped the pass to Jackson, who

TWO-WAY PLAYER

Tim Duncan is the first player in NBA history to be named to both an All-NBA Team and an All-Defensive Team in each of his first eight seasons. Former teammate David Robinson held the previous record, being named in each of his first seven seasons.

calmly swished another three-pointer. The Spurs now had an 80–72 lead, and the loud, deliriously roaring crowd was on its feet.

"Down the stretch, my shot wasn't exactly there and luckily enough I was drawing double teams and those guys were hitting shots," said Duncan. "So I'm going to give them the ball every time they're open."[1]

TIM DUNCAN FILE
Height: 6' 11"
Weight: 260
Date of Birth: April 25, 1976
Position: Power forward
College: Wake Forest University
NBA Team: San Antonio Spurs
Acquired: First overall draft pick, 1997

On the defensive end of the court, Duncan was a disruptive force, taking advantage of his grace and agility to block one shot after another, and it didn't matter where the Nets were shooting the ball. Duncan stuffed a Rodney Rogers layup attempt. Kenyon Martin lofted a seven-foot jumper, only to see Duncan reach up and reject it. Kerry Kittles attempted a twenty-two-foot jumper, but Duncan raced toward Kittles and swatted the ball away. Those three blocked shots were a big reason why the Nets went scoreless on eight straight possessions. Duncan ended the series with an NBA record 32 blocked shots, an average of 5.3 blocks per game.

PLAYING WITH DAVID ROBINSON

When David Robinson, an MVP in 1995, sustained foot and back injuries during the 1996–1997 season, the San Antonio Spurs suffered on the court as the team finished 20-62. It was the third-worst record in the NBA. Thanks to a little luck, the Spurs ended up with the first draft choice and selected Tim Duncan, a power forward out of Wake Forest. With Duncan and Robinson playing together, the Spurs won two titles, including the 2003 title in Robinson's last season. Before the season, Robinson announced it would be his last. Duncan said the goal of the team before the season was to make it a great ending to Robinson's career. Duncan and the rest of the Spurs made that goal come true as San Antonio won the NBA title, allowing Robinson to retire as a champion and close the Tim Duncan-David Robinson chapter on a high note.

By the time the game was over, Duncan had scored 21 points, grabbed 20 rebounds, recorded an NBA Finals-record 8 blocked shots, and dished out 10 assists. More important, his Superman-like performance had given the San Antonio Spurs an 88–77 victory and their second NBA championship.

"I told him he was incredible," said Steve Kerr, who gave Duncan a huge hug when he came out of the game with thirty-five seconds remaining to a thunderous ovation from the fans. "Nothing else needed to be said."[2]

David Robinson, Duncan's retiring teammate, said, "We just always expect a great, great game from him. And he just delivered time and time again. He carried us through almost every time. We just had to provide the help for him."[3]

In the six games against the Nets, Duncan was simply playing at a higher level than everyone else. Despite New Jersey's defensive effort, Duncan averaged 24.2 points per game. Twice in the series he grabbed 20 rebounds in a game. He averaged 17 rebounds for the series.

"I'm sure he had absolutely no clue what his stats were, what was going on statistically," Spurs head coach Gregg Popovich said. "He just knows what's going on in the game and needs to be done."[4]

SUPERSTAR OF THE GAME

The title was not the first for Duncan, and it would not be his last. But the 2003 title may have been the most special.

Duncan was a key player in the Spurs' title run in 1999, but he was only a second-year player. Center David Robinson was the leader of the team. But the 2002–03 year was the final season of Robinson's

THREE-PEAT

Tim Duncan is just the second player in NBA history to earn Finals MVP honors in each of their first three trips to the Finals. Duncan won the award in 1999, 2003, and 2005. He joined Michael Jordan, who was six-for-six in capturing the Finals MVP award.

> **"This [MVP award] is a great honor. . . . I couldn't have won this award without my teammates."**
>
> **—Tim Duncan**

Hall-of-Fame career. Duncan was now the leader of the team, and he did all he could to make sure Robinson's career ended with a title. Duncan's amazing season was rewarded when he was named the league's MVP after averaging 23.3 points, 12.9 rebounds, 3.9 assists, and 2.9 blocks per game. The MVP award was his second straight, and the rebounds, assists, and blocks per game were career highs.

Duncan became only the eighth player in NBA history to win back-to-back MVP honors, joining Bill Russell, Wilt Chamberlain, Kareem Abdul-Jabbar, Moses Malone, Larry Bird, Magic Johnson, and Michael Jordan.

Duncan was now among the giants of the game, a true superstar on the basketball court. But bragging is not a part of Duncan's character. As always, he was more concerned about helping his teammates win than earning awards for himself. As usual, Duncan was humble when asked about becoming an MVP for the second time.

"This [MVP award] is a great honor," Duncan

said. "It's unbeliev-
able to have my name
listed with [the other
back-to-back win-
ners]. They're leg-
ends. I'm just out
here trying to win
games, and I know
I couldn't have won
this award without
my teammates. . . .
At some point,
individual accom-
plishments are
important. I think
you can use them
as goals, you can
use them as you
try to achieve a
certain level. But
no doubt about
it, the [wins] are
the most impor-
tant. The rest of
this has to take
a back seat to
winning. I like
to let that speak for me."[5]

Duncan and the MVP trophy and David
Robinson and the championship trophy

TEAM LEADER

If winning speaks for Duncan, then he was speaking loudly in 2002–2003. Duncan helped lead the Spurs to a franchise-record 60 wins during the regular season. The winning continued in the postseason as San Antonio defeated the Phoenix Suns in the first round of the playoffs, then disposed of the Los Angeles Lakers and Dallas Mavericks before beating the New Jersey Nets in the NBA Finals.

A true measure of greatness is how well a player does in the biggest games. In each of the playoff series-clinching games against the Suns, Lakers, and Mavericks, Duncan was great. Against Phoenix, Duncan had 15 points, 20 rebounds, 10 assists, and 4 blocked shots. Facing the Lakers in Game 6 in the second round, Duncan dropped in 37 points while grab-

TIM DUNCAN'S FIRST SIX SEASONS

Year	Average	Rebounds	Blocked shots	Assists	Steals
1997–1998	21.1	977	206	224	55
1999	21.7	571	126	121	45
1999–2000	23.2	918	165	234	66
2000–2001	22.2	997	192	245	70
2001–2002	25.5	1,042	203	307	61
2002–2003	23.3	1,043	237	316	55

bing 16 rebounds. He also was busy dishing out 4 assists and blocking 2 shots. In Game 6 against Dallas, a 90–78 win that sent the Spurs to the finals, Duncan had 18 points, 11 rebounds, 4 assists, and 3 blocks.

As was the case during the regular season, Duncan was simply unstoppable in the postseason. In twenty-four playoff games, Tim averaged 24.7 points, 15.4 rebounds, 5.3 assists, and 3.3 blocks per game.

That domination on both ends of the court is why Duncan was named the MVP of the NBA Finals, an award he won in 1999 when the Spurs won their first title. That's not bad for a player who would never have played on an NBA court if not for a hurricane that decimated his native Virgin Islands. In fact, Duncan's road to becoming an NBA superstar did not follow a typical track.

A MAN WITH VALUES

Growing up in the Virgin Islands, Duncan enjoyed a quiet, simple life. The values he learned as a child have carried over into adulthood as Duncan has become well known for his charitable way of life.

In 2001, he became even more involved in the community when he created the Tim Duncan Foundation, which is designed to encourage the areas of health awareness and research, education, and youth sports and recreation in San Antonio; Winston-Salem, North Carolina, where Duncan attended Wake Forest University; and the Virgin Islands, where he was born.

Within the Tim Duncan Foundation, Duncan and his wife, Amy, have started several programs, including Tim Duncan's Character Program. It is an educational incentive program that each year rewards 3,000 students from the San Antonio area who show outstanding character traits and also make good choices. The program includes students from kindergarten through the twelfth grade.

Duncan's good deeds, both on the court and off, did not go unnoticed in 2003. In addition to winning the regular season MVP award and the Finals MVP award, Duncan was named the Sportsman of the Year by *The Sporting News*. And in a fitting tribute to his former teammate and mentor, both Duncan and Robinson were named *Sports Illustrated*'s Sportsmen of the Year.

Terry McDonnell, *Sports Illustrated*'s managing editor, said the duo won the award due to what they did both on the court and the way they helped the community.

"They could have won this simply by what they did on the court," McDonnell said. "But behind their athletic contributions, when you look at the language of what this has stood for, it's also been about character and sportsmanship."[6]

2

Growing up on St. Croix

As Tim Duncan jumped into the pool, his long arms and legs allowed him to easily glide through the water. Already tall and lanky, his powerful strokes seemingly lifted Tim out of the water.

It was common to see Tim in the pool, for it was swimming, not basketball, that was his first sport of choice.

Growing up on the island of St. Croix in the U.S. Virgin Islands, Tim was surrounded by water. Located in the Caribbean, St. Croix boasts a very comfortable average temperature of 26 degrees Celsius (79 degrees Fahrenheit). With the waters around the island also comfortably warm, Tim spent hours in the ocean swimming among the vast array of fish and beautiful coral reefs.

NO SHARKS, PLEASE

Growing up on an island, Tim was surrounded by water. While he quickly learned to love the water, he developed a healthy fear of sharks. He is also afraid of heights.

Tim's life growing up could be the basis of a family television show. He was living a nice, quiet life on the island and was surrounded by a loving family and spent time with his friends. His father, Bill, was a strict parent, but he loved his children as much as any father.

Tim's mother, Ione, nurtured her son and his two older sisters, Cheryl and Tricia. Ione was the rock of the family, the parent Tim turned to for support. Bill and Ione provided a solid foundation that carried over into adulthood. They taught their children to be self-reliant, stressed academics, and encouraged them in their athletic endeavors.

GIFTED SWIMMER

Swimming was a way of life for the Duncans. Cheryl was one of the top swimmers on the island and was very competitive in high school before graduating and becoming a nurse. Then there was Tricia.

She was not just one of the top swimmers on the island; she may be one of the best swimmers ever from St. Croix. Excelling at the highest level in the backstroke, Tricia was selected to the United States swim team for the 1988 Summer Olympics.

Because of his upbringing, Tim was very close to his sisters, especially Tricia. Her trip to the Olympics did not result in a medal, but her success left an impression on Tim and guided him to the pool.

Soon, those leisurely swims in the ocean were replaced by one lap after another, stroke after stroke, in the pool. The long days of training quickly resulted in success.

Taking the blocks at a swim meet, Tim sprang into the water. Reaching out with his long arms and kicking with his long legs, Tim left a streak of white foam behind him. Also left behind him was the rest of the competition. Soon, Tim was piling up the victories, and always on hand was his mother.

She was there in the stands, shouting encouragement to Tricia and Tim. For years, she tirelessly spent hours driving her children to swim practice and meets. She served as a volunteer with the timers when asked to help. If Tim was feeling any pressure to succeed in the pool and match his sister's accomplishments or not let his mother down, he never showed it.

LATE BLOOMER

With swimming being such a big part of his life as a child, Tim did not start playing organized basketball until he was in the ninth grade.

"I don't think it [pressure] exists for him," said Michael Lohberg, Tim's former swimming coach. "He creates his own world."[1]

At the age of thirteen, Tim was one of the top swimmers in the four-hundred-meter freestyle. Everyone believed he would be the next great Olympic swimmer from the Virgin Islands.

"As a swimmer, Tim Duncan could have been tremendous," said Tim's longtime friend, Rashidi Clenance. "That's when the Virgin Islands first got a glimpse of Tim Duncan the athlete. I always tell people that Tim Duncan could have been famous either way."[2]

STANDING OUT

Tim wasn't always the world-class athlete many perceive him to be today. Instead, he really didn't fit in with many of his

> **"As a swimmer, Tim Duncan could have been tremendous. That's when the Virgin Islands first got a glimpse of Tim Duncan the athlete. I always tell people that Tim Duncan could have been famous either way."**
>
> **—friend, Rashidi Clenance**

classmates. Taller than the rest of the kids his age, Tim was made fun of by the other kids.

"I knew him as a tall kid that wasn't in the popular group," Clenance said. "As kids, part of becoming accepted is by making another kid feel rejected. He [Tim] stood out. He was much bigger than the rest of us. Some guys were real cruel to him."[3]

VIDEO PLAYER

Tim Duncan is still a big kid at heart. When not playing basketball, he can often be found playing video games, something he says is his worst habit. When not playing video games, he is often sitting in front of the computer surfing the Internet.

SPORTS OFFERS MORE THAN EXERCISE

Being involved in athletics all of his life, Tim Duncan has experienced first-hand the benefits of participating in athletic events. The obvious benefit of being active in swimming or playing basketball or any other sport is that it helps the athlete stay in shape. But Duncan also believes basketball, or any sport, can help prepare kids for the real world. Duncan believes sports teach dedication because a child is required to practice and work hard to achieve a goal. Duncan also said playing basketball has helped him learn how to work with others and be selfless. A third benefit of playing a sport, Duncan believes, is that it teaches camaraderie. By playing on a team, a child comes into contact with all types of personalities and cultures. Duncan said that helped him appreciate differences in other people.

Tim didn't allow any of those taunts and jeers suffered during his early childhood to affect him. He remembered what his parents had taught him: the importance of being self-reliant and confident in oneself. In fact, those taunts may be why Tim is the dedicated and hard-working athlete he is today. Any anger he may have felt was released during his training in the pool, allowing him to push himself individually to become the best swimmer he could become.

Swimming, for the most part, is a solitary sport. There are no teammates to help you out in the pool. In order to improve, Tim has said that he needed to drive himself, to find a work ethic, and drive within himself to become good. That work ethic has carried over into his professional life.

JURASSIC PARK

Tim Duncan's favorite books as a child were the *Encyclopedia Brown* series, but now he claims that *Jurassic Park* is his favorite book.

Tim has always worked hard in practice, spending hours honing his skills. His nickname is Big Fundamental because of his mastery of the basic skills needed in basketball, from footwork to his soft, feathery shot.

But hard work alone is not why Tim has become a Most Valuable Player in the National Basketball Association. Tim's days as a swimmer provided him the foundation around which to build his skills.

Tim had to use all of his muscles in concert with each other when he was a competitive swimmer. His arms and legs moved together like a well-oiled machine. His back muscles worked in unison with the shoulders and hamstrings, giving him a certain amount of grace and balance in the pool.

That grace and balance is seen today when the Spurs take the court. Tim's footwork in the lane can be traced back to his days in the swimming pool. His ability to run the court is a tribute to the endurance he needed to be a top swimmer.

Duncan makes a layup in the 2003 Western Conference Finals.

But Tim's decision to become a basketball player was not one he made on his own. Instead, his journey to the NBA may never have happened if not for a tragic event in his life and the lives of those in the Virgin Islands.

CHAPTER THREE

A Life Changed Forever

The horrific wind was howling outside the Duncan household as Hurricane Hugo was tearing through the Virgin Islands in September of 1989. While Tim and the rest of his family huddled in a bathroom surrounded by a strong cinder-block wall, Hugo was ripping trees right out of the ground, flinging them like they were matchsticks.

The massive gusts of wind ripped one roof after another off houses. Hugo eventually moved on, but it left behind a wake of destruction. About the only home that didn't suffer damage was Tim's house, thanks to the building skills of his father, Bill. He'd tirelessly worked on the house. Bill nearly doubled the home's size, and he'd built it to withstand hurricane-force winds.

Thirteen-year-old Tim and the rest of his family escaped the storm unscathed, but Tim's life would forever be changed by Hugo's harmful path. Nearly every swimming pool on St. Croix was damaged or destroyed, including the only Olympic-sized pool on the island.

Tim had a choice to make. He could continue to train by swimming in the ocean, or he could end his swimming career. Afraid of sharks, Tim decided swimming was no longer in his future.

"Tim was not happy about swim-ming in the ocean," said his father, Bill. "He was afraid of the sharks. He did what I would do and got out."[1]

Sailboats beached by Hurricane Hugo litter a street on St. Croix.

Just like that, Tim's plan for the future was altered. With the pool he trained in wiped out, his dreams of swimming in the Olympics, as his sister Tricia did, were wiped out as well. To this day, many people believe Tim would have been an Olympic swimmer if not for Hugo. Tim himself has said he doesn't know if he would have ever played basketball if Hugo had never hit the Virgin Islands.

CHANGING SPORTS

Without swimming, Tim had a competitive void to fill. After he entered St. Dunstan's Episcopal High School, Tim needed to compete in a sport. He started to play basketball. Having never picked up a basketball, Tim was not very good on the hardwood.

But there was nothing else for him to turn to. With the pool destroyed and sharks in the ocean, he could not return to swimming. So he stuck to basketball. And always wanting to improve, he turned to Ricky Lowery, Cheryl's husband, for help.

Though he remained clumsy on the court, Tim was already the tallest player in his class, allowing him to overcome his awkwardness. He just needed help refining his skills, and that is where Lowery, who is like a brother to Tim, came in.

A former guard at Capital University, a small Division III school in Columbus, Ohio, Lowery helped Tim develop into the player he is today. The duo first started playing against each other one-on-one. Lowery then had Tim playing in pickup games.

When alone, Lowery often made his pupil go through a variety of drills, including dribbling a basketball on stones or up and down stairs. Lowery also taught Tim to pass and handle the ball like a guard, develop a soft shot from the outside, and use his left hand as well as his right to score in the paint, traits you can see when watching Tim play for the Spurs.

LATE BLOOMER

Tim Duncan wears number 21 for the Spurs in honor of his brother-in-law, Ricky Lowery, who helped Tim learn the game of basketball. Lowery wore number 21 in college when he played for Capital University.

NOTHING WRONG WITH COMIC BOOKS

While Tim didn't start playing basketball until he was in the ninth grade, he had numerous interests outside of sports, such as playing video games. But Tim also spent hours of his time collecting comic books. During his childhood on St. Croix, Tim loved to read a variety of comic books. They would take him to another world, one of superheroes and lands very different from his own. One of Tim's favorite comic book superheroes is Wolverine from the *X-Men*, a comic book series he really enjoyed reading. For years, comic books have been turned into movies. Tim's favorite movie, *The Crow,* originally was a comic book. Tim said he is drawn to the character because of his anti-hero storyline.

MAGIC MAN

Tim's favorite basketball player growing up was Magic Johnson of the Los Angeles Lakers. When Tim first played for his high school, he played point guard and tried to incorporate what Johnson did for the Lakers into his own game.

Another trait that is easy to spot when watching Tim today is his approach to the game. Always a thinker, Tim is able to understand situations seemingly before they even happen. Very seldom does an opponent outthink Tim on the court. He developed this skill while learning the game from Lowery.

At the same time, Tim continued to grow. By his senior year at St. Dunstan's, Tim was six feet ten inches and a force on the court. When down low in the paint, Tim used his size to dominate opponents. But because of the skills he learned from Lowery, he was able to dribble the ball up the court, pass out of double-teams with ease, or hit a short jumper. Basically, Tim was the total package and the best player anyone in the Virgin Islands had ever seen.

A HUGE LOSS

Unfortunately for Tim, his mother never got to see her son develop into a great basketball player. The day before Tim was to turn fourteen and only seven months after Hugo tore through the Virgin Islands, Ione died of breast cancer.

It was a devastating blow to Tim and his sisters. Their biggest cheerleader was gone. Tim learned of his mother's death from his father. After he told the news to Tricia, who began sobbing in her bedroom, Tim walked into the living room and plopped in front of the television. For the rest of the day, he played video games, keeping whatever feelings he had to himself.

His birthday came the next day, but there was no celebration. It was lost, perhaps even forgotten, in the grieving process. Tim was suddenly forced to change his view of life. No longer was everything always going to be fine. First he had to live through the destruction of Hurricane Hugo. Then he had to learn how to live without his mother.

"I've been grown-up for a long time," Tim once said. "I went through that with my mom, and I grew to where I understood life and death and everything

ABOUT THE VIRGIN ISLANDS

The Virgin Islands were explored by Christopher Columbus in 1493. Soon after, Spanish forces claimed the islands as their territory. The United States purchased the islands from Spain in 1917, and they are considered a commonwealth of the United States. Because of that, Tim Duncan is a United States citizen and allowed to play for the United States in the Olympics and other international competitions.

in between. It does make you realize your own mortality and the mortality of the people around you. You understand that you're not going to be around forever. You're not invincible."[2]

Before Ione died, she made Tim promise to graduate from college. She wanted to make sure her son made something of himself. Duncan did not want to let his mother down, and it was not in Tim's character to sulk or pout.

Tim remembered a nursery rhyme his mother would recite to him before bed. "Good, Better, Best. Never let it rest. Until your Good is Better, and your Better is your Best." Those are words that Tim has remembered his entire life, and they are words he used to get over his mother's death. Turning to the self-reliance instilled in him by his parents, Tim poured himself into basketball, soaking up whatever Lowery and his coaches would teach him, while also maintaining his grades in school.

GAINING ATTENTION

News of Tim's exploits on the court soon reached the United States. Coaches from many colleges had come to St. Croix to see if Tim was the real thing. He was averaging 25 points per game and simply dominating his opponents.

But most of the coaches on hand were from smaller colleges that could take a chance on a player

Duncan jams the ball for Wake Forest in 1997.

BOARD, NOT BORED
When not playing video games or surfing the Internet, Tim likes to play board games. His favorite board game is Monopoly.

like Tim. For while he was head and shoulders better than anyone on the court, his competition was relatively weak.

Schools such as North Carolina and Duke were not recruiting Tim. That was good news for Wake Forest, a small school located in Winston-Salem, North Carolina. While always competitive in the Atlantic Coast Conference, the Demon Deacons were still in the shadow of neighbors Duke and North Carolina.

Most of all, Duncan wanted a college degree, to fulfill his promise to his mother.

But good fortune was shining on Wake Forest. Former Demon Deacon player Chris King played in the Virgin Islands during an NBA goodwill tour and visited St. Croix. When King returned to North Carolina, Dave Odom, Wake Forest's coach at the time, just happened to ask King if he saw any players who he thought could play college basketball. King didn't know Tim's name, but he gave a glowing appraisal of Tim's ability to play.

"He said, 'Coach, there was a kid down there who played pretty well against Alonzo,'" Odom said. "I said, 'Alonzo Mourning?' I put one of my crack assistants on it, and I promise you in two days we had his name, his home number, his island, his school and his coach's number.

"And I had my plane ticket, fairly quickly."[3]

Odom was soon on St. Croix watching Tim play on an outdoor court. It was a recruiting trip Odom describes as a nice afternoon. He loved what he saw on the court. He knew Tim would be heavily recruited if he played in the United States.

But Odom was also impressed with Tim's character as a person, the way he conducted himself away from the court. Tim had already dealt with two tragedies in his life, but both failed to sidetrack him from his goals. In fact, they seemed to have strengthened his drive to succeed.

Tim was also polite and listened to advice. And most of all, he wanted a college degree, to fulfill his promise to his mother. Soon, Tim would be on his way to Winston-Salem, and on his way to college stardom.

CHAPTER FOUR

Settling in at Wake Forest

While Odom played a large role in persuading Duncan to attend Wake Forest, the academic side of the school left Duncan impressed as well. He was fully intent on getting his college degree and keeping his promise to his mother.

But Duncan wanted more than just his name on a degree. He wanted a real education and put as much effort into learning as he did into playing basketball. Duncan didn't avoid tough classes. He felt the challenge of a hard class would only help him improve as a student. Always considered an intellectual thinker and a person who liked to study others, Duncan was drawn to the school's Psychology Department and decided to major in psychology.

While Duncan adjusted to life in the classroom, adjusting to life on the basketball court was a little more difficult. He experienced a series of ups and downs during his freshman season.

His skill was easy to see. The ability to dribble, pass, rebound, play defense, and shoot did not disappear during the move from St. Croix to Winston-Salem. In simple terms, he was a raw talent. During fall workouts, however, he was so impressive he was named a starter as a freshman. His desire to improve on the basketball court and adjust to college life helped earn Duncan a starting spot. "The first drills he did, I thought, 'This guy needs work,'" Odom

ARE YOU SAYING SOMETHING?

As Tim Duncan got better and better at Wake Forest, opposing players and fans did their best to rattle him more and more. But nothing ever worked. No matter what was said to Duncan on the court, he never showed any response. There was no sign of anger. Soon, people began to call him Spock—like the "Star Trek" character—because he showed no emotion off the court. But what people forgot was that Duncan was a psychology major. By being silent, by keeping control of his emotions, he knew it would be opposing players and fans who would get rattled instead of him. "You destroy people's psyches when you do that," Duncan says. "You absolutely destroy them. They can't get inside your head. They're talking to you, and there's no response other than to make this shot, make this play, get this rebound and go the other way. People hate that."

said. "But he learned faster than anyone I've ever coached. A lot of kids don't like college, and they are looking for a way to get out of it. The converse was true with Tim. He enjoyed college, throwing the Frisbee™, being with his fellow students and studying psychology. He was very aware that his family and, in particular, his mother, had encouraged him to get his education."[1]

WORKING TO IMPROVE

While Duncan was blending in well at Wake Forest, facing older, stronger, and bigger players on the basketball court was tough on him. In his very first game as a collegian, Duncan, who averaged 25 points per game as a senior in high school, failed to score. He looked overmatched at times against players who were sometimes four years older than he was.

But the coaching staff knew Duncan would get better. They knew he would adjust to the challenge of facing older and stronger opponents. Duncan quickly showed why he was starting as a

BACKWARD SHORTS

Duncan wears his practice shorts backwards, a superstition that started at Wake Forest. After wearing his shorts backwards at one practice, he had a great game and has thus continued the practice habit to this day.

freshman when, in only his second game, he recorded his first double-double at Wake Forest by scoring 12 points and grabbing 12 rebounds.

Duncan continued to experience his ups and downs during the 1993-94 season, but there were more highs than lows. By the end of the season, he was a solid contributor on the court. Playing 30 minutes per game, Duncan averaged 9.8 points and 9.6 rebounds in thirty-three games. Duncan also shot an impressive 55 percent from the field, and many of those shots came on short to mid-range jumpers, not on layups and slam dunks in the lane.

Duncan hangs from the rim after dunking a shot against Maryland.

But Duncan was not a one-dimensional player. Defensively, Duncan blocked 3.8 shots per game and had just under one assist per game. Those numbers, however, were just the tip of the iceberg of what was to come.

SOPHOMORE SEASON

As a sophomore, Duncan took a huge step forward. He was too tall for most forwards to guard effectively. He was too quick for centers to defend, as he would beat them off the dribble game after game.

Teammates looked for Duncan to score more often, and he came through for them by averaging 16.8 points, hitting 59 percent of his shots. But he also improved in every facet of the game. Using his quickness and strong leaping ability, he grabbed 12.5 rebounds per game to lead the Atlantic Coast Conference. He also led the ACC in blocked shots with 4.2 per game and became the school's all-time leader in blocked shots.

As the season progressed, more and more opposing coaches were trying to figure out how to stop the big Demon Deacon. But nothing seemed to work. When the season ended, the awards rolled in for Duncan. He was named a third-team All-American and was a first-team ACC selection.

Duncan was simply getting better and better, helping Wake Forest win more and more. For Duncan, winning was even more important than the impressive numbers he was recording. Wake Forest reached a No. 3 national ranking in the Associated Press poll and won the ACC tournament, finishing the season with 26 wins.

In the NCAA tournament, Duncan helped Wake

Forest reach the Sweet 16 by leading the Demon Deacons to victories against North Carolina A&T and St. Louis before falling to Oklahoma State.

After his sophomore season, there was no longer any doubt about how good Duncan was. But Duncan didn't want to be just good. He strived to be the best he could, to be great. Settling for just being good was not in Duncan's character. With his mastery of the fundamental skills, his ability to hit the bank shot and short jumpers, he was already better than most players offensively. But he knew it would not be enough.

ADDING TO HIS SKILLS

So during the summer, he worked on a hook shot to take better advantage of his height. He also worked on a step-back jump shot to create more room between him and the defender. The more offensive weapons a defender had to think about, the easier it would be for Duncan to score.

Just as he improved from his freshman to sophomore season, Duncan was even better during his third year at Wake Forest, despite the fact opposing defenses were designed to stop him. Duncan scored 19.1 points per game and made 55.5

THE BANK IS OPEN

Duncan prefers to shoot the bank shot. He says it is more comfortable for him to shoot the ball off the backboard instead of shooting directly at the rim of the basket from an angle.

percent of his shots, making a career-high 228 shots. His work on his shooting range during the off-season also resulted in a career-high 7 three-pointers, which is not bad for a seven-footer.

But Duncan didn't just shoot the ball better from farther out on the court. With zone defenses surrounding him, Duncan knew the team would often have a better chance of scoring if he passed the ball instead of hoisting up a bad shot. With his teammates taking advantage of the open shots he created by drawing the attention of opposing defenders, Duncan ended the season with a career-high 93 assists, an average of 2.9 per game.

Riding Duncan's amazing skills, Wake Forest again won twenty-six games and claimed the ACC tournament title. In the ACC championship game against Georgia Tech, Duncan led the Demon Deacons to a 75–74 victory by scoring 27 points and grabbing 22 rebounds, the most ever in an ACC title game. His 56 rebounds in three games is also an ACC tournament record. Duncan's awe-inspiring skills drew accolades from opposing coaches and players.

"Tim Duncan is what I call the total package," Georgia Tech head coach Bobby Cremins said.[2]

> ## "Tim Duncan is what I call the total package."
>
> **—Georgia Tech head coach Bobby Cremins**

Duncan dunks the ball during an ACC conference game in 1996.

Said North Carolina State center Todd Fuller: "Each time out playing against him, he adds his own little twist to his game. He's an incredible player. It's a challenge going up against a player like that."[3]

Duncan's play lifted Wake Forest to the Elite Eight of the NCAA tournament. The Demon Deacons defeated Northeast Louisiana in the opening round of the tournament. Then came two close wins—a 65–62 victory against Texas and a 60–59 win against Louisville—to send Wake Forest to the Elite Eight. Eventual national champion Kentucky ended the Demon Deacons' season with an 83–63 win.

While the Wake Forest season came to an end with the loss to Kentucky, Duncan was unable to escape the spotlight as fans and scouts wondered what he would do next. Would he go to the NBA or stay in college?

KEEPING HIS PROMISE

Considering what he had done already at Wake Forest, there was no doubt he would be the first player taken in the draft if he decided to skip his senior year of college. Millions of dollars were within his grasp.

But NBA teams were wasting their time

JUNIOR YEAR

During his junior season, Duncan averaged 22.7 points and an amazing 18.7 rebounds per game during the ACC postseason tournament to lead Wake Forest to their second straight league title.

TIM DUNCAN'S CAREER AT WAKE FOREST

Year	Average	Rebounds	Blocked shots	Assists	Steals
1993–1994	9.8	317	124	30	12
1994–1995	16.8	401	135	67	13
1995–1996	19.1	395	120	93	22
1996–1997	20.8	457	102	98	22

and energy waiting for Duncan to make a decision, because there was never really a decision to make. Duncan was determined to keep the promise he made to his mother and earn a college degree. If he left school early, the chances of earning that degree would be greatly reduced.

Duncan still had unfinished business to attend to as well. He had a strong desire to lead Wake Forest to the national title. They had accomplished so much as a team, but winning a title was the one goal that had not been reached during his first three years as a Demon Deacon.

The NBA was going to have to wait for Duncan to graduate and earn his degree. That is what his mother wanted, and that is what Duncan was going to get.

CHAPTER FIVE

Staying Paves Way to NBA Stardom

After Duncan's junior season, people were questioning why he was willing to pass up millions of dollars by staying in school. He was a certain lottery pick and perhaps would have been the top pick in the draft.

But Duncan knew he needed more experience if he wanted to succeed immediately on the professional level. Because his birthday, April 25, 1976, was so late in the school year, he was only twenty years old. According to Duncan, remaining at Wake Forest for his senior season made him stronger, smarter, and better prepared for life after college.

From the outset of the 1996–97 season, Duncan was clearly the best player on the floor in every game he played. With another off-season to work on his game, there was nothing he couldn't do during his senior season.

A FAN TOO

While attending Wake Forest, Duncan enjoyed other Demon Deacon sporting events and cheered for the other athletes, many of whom were his friends.

The fluid motion he developed as a swimmer carried over to the basketball court and allowed him to run the floor like a small forward. His strength allowed him to get great position in the paint and produce easy shots. His hard work developing his jump shot enabled him to step outside and score as well. His height and explosiveness allowed him to be a top rebounder and shot blocker.

In a game against Maryland, Wake Forest trailed by 12 points at halftime. Knowing he had to lead the team, Duncan took control of the game in the second half, putting his entire game on display. A bank shot

MRS. DUNCAN

Duncan met his future wife, Amy, while attending Wake Forest University.

here and a short jumper there and soon the lead was cut in half. Duncan scored on hook

NUMBER RETIRED

No basketball player at Wake Forest will ever wear No. 21 again, as the Demon Deacons have retired the number in Duncan's honor.

shots, turn-around jumpers, and layups. During the final 20 minutes of action, he scored 25 points to lead the Demon Deacons to victory.

Duncan averaged 20.8 points for the season and led the nation in rebounding, averaging 14.7 per game. Duncan was so effective on offense, he made nearly 61 percent of his shots while still dishing out a career-high 3.2 assists per game. The only thing Duncan couldn't do was lead Wake Forest to the national title—the Demon Deacons lost to Stanford in the second round of the NCAA tournament.

By the end of the season, Duncan's impressive numbers landed him one award after another. He was the Associated Press Player of the Year and won the Naismith and Wooden awards as the top player in college basketball. For the third consecutive season, he was voted the National Association of Basketball Coaches Defensive Player of the Year.

Duncan finished his career with 481 blocked shots, the most in ACC history and second all-time in NCAA history. He was only the tenth player in NCAA Division I history to score 2,000 points and grab 1,500 rebounds in his career. No one could question whether he was the best player in college basketball.

The only question as far as his basketball future was concerned was where he would play. Which team would win the lottery and earn the top pick in the draft and get the chance to have Duncan become the anchor of the team?

After Wake Forest's season came to an end, Duncan's schedule remained as hectic as ever. There was no time to rest and relax. While trying to graduate from school, he was also working hard on the basketball court in order to keep improving his game.

Duncan and his father are introduced at Duncan's last home game in 1997.

NBA LOTTERY

When the NBA regular season comes to a close, the teams that do not make the playoffs are placed into a lottery, in which each team is assigned a certain percentage of lottery balls based on its final place in the standings. The team with the worst record has a better chance of landing the top pick than the team with the tenth worst record.

Because the Vancouver Grizzlies were ineligible to get the top pick as part of their agreement for entering the NBA as an expansion team, the Boston Celtics had the highest percentage of landing the top pick. Doing so would have meant landing Duncan. But the Philadelphia 76ers and the Spurs were also coming off tough seasons, with San Antonio going 20–62 in the 1996–97 season.

The weeks leading up to the draft were chaotic. Duncan headed home to be surrounded by his friends and family. Returning to St. Croix allowed Duncan time to step away from basketball, if only for a little while, and relax.

Sitting in his living room, Duncan and his family were riveted to the television as the order of the draft was unfolding on national television. The Celtics, the team with the best chance of landing the top pick, ran into bad luck. They were slotted into the third position. Duncan now knew that he was either headed to Philadelphia or San Antonio.

The next few seconds seemed to last for hours as the anticipation in Duncan's living room increased. When the logo of the 76ers was unveiled in the number two spot in the draft, Duncan finally knew where

Duncan and NBA
Commissioner David Stern

OFF TO THE ROOKIE LEAGUES

After the draft and before the start of training camp, the various teams in the NBA send players to participate in a rookie league. The teams are usually a collection of second-round draft choices who need more work on the court, or undrafted free agents who are looking to prove they are good enough to play in the NBA.

Spurs head coach Gregg Popovich, however, wanted Duncan to play in a rookie league, an unusual request to ask of the top pick in the draft. Duncan, however, quickly agreed to the request. If playing in a rookie league meant he would improve, then that is what he was going to do.

That summer before the start of the 1997–98 season, Duncan understood his strength was shooting the ball and rebounding. So instead of concentrating on scoring, Duncan made sure he worked on his passing and ball-handling skills, further enhancing his all-around skills.

he was headed—to San Antonio. When the draft finally came around, the Spurs made it official when they selected Duncan with the top pick. All of the hard, grueling workouts on the basketball court and in the weight room had paid off.

"That was a great day," Duncan said. "It is an amazing feeling to have that honor [of being the top draft pick], but the days and weeks leading up to the draft were somewhat nerve-wracking because you didn't really know what was going to happen on draft day or where your new home may be. There were so many things going on in my head, but overall it is a great memory."[1]

NEW TOWN, NEW TEAM

Duncan wasn't able to celebrate for long. Soon after the draft, his career with the Spurs began unfolding, and Duncan had to adjust to a new life in a new city. While San Antonio is not a bustling city like New York, Chicago, or Los Angeles, it has more than one million residents.

That is a far cry from the peaceful surroundings Duncan grew up with in St. Croix or even Winston-Salem. After four years of stability at Wake Forest, Duncan had to find a place to live and get acquainted with a whole new set of teammates.

But Duncan was joining a team that had two-time MVP David Robinson on the roster. Being drafted by San Antonio and playing next to Robinson would allow Duncan to thrive. It was a perfect marriage of student and pupil.

ALL-TIMER

Duncan was voted onto the Atlantic Coast Conference Fiftieth Anniversary Basketball Team. A 120-member committee selected the fifty-member team. Duncan was one of five former Wake Forest players to be named to the team.

CHAPTER SIX

Rookie of the Year

It was opening night, Duncan's first official game as a professional, and the San Antonio fans were ready to watch their top draft pick's debut. The arena was bustling with electricity as fans were ready to see what Duncan would be able to do.

The Spurs were facing the Denver Nuggets, who were trotting out their own highly touted rookie, Bobby Jackson. The two rookies put on a display on the basketball court. There was Jackson, darting between defenders for easy baskets or shooting over them from the outside. By the end of the night, Jackson had 27 points.

But Duncan was by no means a disappointment in his debut. In fact, he put on a show in which he did exactly what the Spurs needed him to do. Coming out relaxed and determined to fit into the flow of the game, Duncan scored 15 points and snatched 10 rebounds. Most important to Duncan, he helped lead the Spurs to a 107–96 victory.

With Robinson still the focus of the offense, Duncan was able to quickly but quietly adjust to the NBA. Duncan was able to feed off Robinson and watch how he fought for position in the paint or how he defended certain players. Duncan not only showed

Duncan congratulates Robinson for making a big play.

skill on the court, but knowledge of the game. Instead of getting into situations that would hurt the team, he avoided needless fouls. Day by day, Duncan was learning how to be a success in the NBA.

A STRING OF BAD LUCK

Winning the lottery allowed San Antonio to add Duncan to its team. But as it turned out, Duncan won the lottery by landing with the Spurs. Yes, the team had struggled the previous season, but not because the team was bad.

San Antonio had a string of seven consecutive winning seasons from 1989–90 to 1995–96. With David Robinson leading the way, the Spurs averaged nearly 55 wins per season and made the playoffs in four consecutive seasons before stumbling in 1996–97. Everything that could go wrong for San Antonio during that season did go wrong.

Robinson missed significant time due to foot and back problems. He played in only six of the team's eighty-two games. The injury bug also hit Sean Elliott, Chuck Person, and Charles Smith. Elliott played in only thirty-nine games, while Person missed the entire season. Smith played in only nineteen games in what would be his final season in the NBA.

THE ROOKIE AND THE VETERAN

After the draft, Duncan immediately realized he was lucky to be with the Spurs. Most No. 1 picks in the draft spend the next season on a team trying to rebuild. But by being with the Spurs, Duncan understood the team would be able to win a lot of games during his rookie season.

Of course, it helps when you have a healthy Robinson, who was one of the best players in the league, back at 100 percent. Soon after the two seven-footers met, they were together all the time. Practicing against each other, they each learned new moves and made each other better.

Duncan has said it was very beneficial to watch Robinson's training regimen and learn from a player who had so much success in the NBA. By watching Robinson, Duncan knew what it would take to become a winner.

JOKESTER

While displaying a quiet and reserved personality, Duncan loves to play practical jokes on both his teammates and coaches.

Robinson said he was impressed with Duncan's attitude from the first time they practiced together. Unlike other top draft picks, Duncan was there to work hard, and, most important, he was open to learning from others.

Soon, the rookie and the veteran were best friends as Robinson played the role of mentor to Duncan. It was easy to see why they got along. Both

Duncan and Robinson were quiet, preferring to share the spotlight instead of steal it. Robinson, just like Duncan, cared only about winning. Personal achievement was sought only to help the team win, not to gain fame and fortune.

There could have been a problem on the court and in the locker room, since both Robinson and Duncan were centers. But Robinson was the team's leader and its center. Duncan understood that, and without hesitation, he moved to the power forward position. Making the transition was not a problem for Duncan.

After flying to St. Croix to meet his newest player, Gregg Popovich, the Spurs' head coach, knew Duncan wouldn't have any difficulty with a change of position. "He's basically an introverted, quite humorous, highly intelligent, easygoing guy who has gotten over himself," Popovich said. "He's not that impressed with himself. He just likes playing ball, and he goes home and does whatever he does. That's him."[1]

SHOWCASING HIS TALENT

Duncan wasted little time showing how good he could be. In a preseason game against the Houston Rockets, Duncan scored 17 points and grabbed 17 rebounds. He showed he could do well in the NBA, but that was the preseason, when teams don't really put together game plans and often put players on the

Duncan prepares to shoot against the Grizzlies at GM Place in Vancouver, Canada, December 30, 1997.

floor who are trying to win jobs, not veterans who know they will be with the team.

Duncan came out strong on opening night against the Nuggets and continued to play well the rest of the season. In November, Duncan set a Spurs rookie record with 22 rebounds against the Chicago Bulls. In December, barely two months into the season, Duncan had his first 30-point game, showing off his vast array of shots.

WHAT A ROOKIE YEAR

Just how good was Tim Duncan during his rookie season? It was one of the best ever. Duncan was voted the league's Rookie of the Month for all six months of the season. Only Ralph Sampson in 1984 and teammate David Robinson in 1990 had swept the monthly awards. Duncan ranked thirteenth in the league in scoring with 21.1 points per game and was third in rebounding, averaging 11.9. Duncan was only the nineteenth rookie in NBA history to average more than 20 points and 10 rebounds per game. His 2.5 blocks per game ranked sixth in the league. He was fourth in the league with a .549 shooting percentage. In a league that included Shaquille O'Neal, Hakeem Olajuwon, and David Robinson, it was Duncan who led the NBA in double-doubles with 57.

That game was just the beginning of a breakout stretch for Duncan. Over the next fourteen games, he averaged 20 points and close to 12 rebounds per game. Duncan was so impressive during the first half of the season that he was named to the All-Star team.

Duncan was the first rookie since Grant Hill in 1995 to play in the All-Star game. Surrounded by scorers, Duncan didn't look to put the ball in the basket. He took only 4 shots and hit one to finish with 2 points. Instead, he concentrated on defense, to do the hard work. In fourteen minutes of play, Duncan grabbed 11 rebounds, tying for game-high honors.

With Duncan paired with Robinson, the Spurs

were winning games at their usual clip once again. But toward the end of the season, with playoff seeding on the line, the Spurs lost the services of Robinson for three games after he suffered a concussion.

For Duncan, it was time to prove he could perform without Robinson by his side. As always, Duncan came through when his teammates needed him most. He averaged 28.7 points and 14.3 rebounds per game. More importantly, San Antonio won all three games while Robinson was on the bench. Instead of getting tired toward the end of the season, a trait often experienced by rookies, Duncan was only getting better and better. He finished the year by scoring in double figures in each of his final fifty-two games.

By the end of the regular season, San Antonio won fifty-six games, an improvement of thirty-six games, an NBA record, from the previous season. A big reason for that was Duncan. There was no doubt he would be named the Rookie of the Year, but the voting wasn't even close. He was voted first on 113 of the 116 ballots. His landslide victory was the largest since Shaquille O'Neal garnered 98 percent of the first-place votes after the 1992–93 season.

Duncan was happy to be the Rookie of the Year, but he didn't get too carried away with the honor.

"It's a goal I had coming into this year," Duncan said. "I wanted to play well this year and win this award.

Duncan holds up his NBA Rookie of the Year trophy.

It's been great playing with every one of my teammates because it's a veteran crew. I came in here with little pressure on me because we had such a core of great players."[2]

DOUBLE-DOUBLE
During his first eight seasons in the NBA, Duncan led the league in double-doubles with 445 in 586 games.

Popovich was impressed with Duncan before the season, and was equally impressed by his big rookie at the end of the season. "He's big time, just like David [Robinson] was and just like Shaq was," Popovich said. "His demeanor and approach to this whole business is uncommon and extraordinary."[3]

SAN ANTONIO'S RECORD IN DUNCAN'S FIRST EIGHT SEASONS

YEAR	WINS	LOSSES	PERCENTAGE
2004–05	59	23	.720
2003–04	57	25	.695
2002–03	60	22	.732
2001–02	58	24	.707
2000–01	58	24	.707
1999–00	53	29	.646
1998–99	37	13	.740
1997–98	56	26	.683

GOING TO THE PLAYOFFS

AMONG LEGENDS

Duncan is just the fifth player in league history to earn All-NBA First Team honors in each of his first eight seasons, joining Elgin Baylor (first 10 seasons), Bob Petit (10), Larry Bird (9), and Oscar Robertson (9).

But the season was not over for the Spurs. Next up were the Phoenix Suns in the first round of the playoffs. The Suns, one of the hottest teams in the league during the second half of the season, edged San Antonio for the fourth seed in the playoffs, meaning they had home-court advantage against the Spurs.

If Duncan was nervous playing in his first NBA postseason, he sure didn't show it. In fact, he looked like a seasoned veteran. In the first game against the Suns in Phoenix, Duncan scored 32 points. With the game on the line in the fourth quarter, the Rookie of the Year became the focal point of the offense.

One bucket led to another. The Suns were guarding Duncan with only one defender, and the strategy backfired as he scored 12 straight points. By the end of the quarter, Duncan tallied 18 points in that twelve-minute span to lead the Spurs to a 102–96 victory.

By claiming a crucial win on the road, the Spurs took home-court advantage away from Phoenix. San

Antonio never gave it back. After losing Game 2, the Spurs won Games 3 and 4 to claim a 3–1 series win.

Facing the top-seeded Utah Jazz in the second round, the Spurs didn't experience the same success they had against the Suns. Utah won the series four games to one, but nearly every game was close. The Jazz won the first game 83–82 and then escaped the second game with a 109–106 win in overtime. During that game, Duncan suffered a sprained ankle that slowed him down the rest of the series.

Still, Duncan ended the playoffs averaging a team-best 20.7 points while making 52 percent of his shots. He ranked second behind Robinson in rebounding, grabbing 9 per game, and blocked shots, with 2.56 per game.

In the end, the Jazz proved to be the better team. But the Spurs learned they could compete with the best teams in the league. The 1998 playoffs were a precursor of what was to come in 1999.

CHAPTER SEVEN

Just Call Him Champ

The sound was deafening as the fans inside Madison Square Garden were cheering wildly in the final minute of Game 5 of the 1999 NBA Finals. The Knicks were less than fifty seconds from pulling to within one game of the San Antonio Spurs.

The Spurs were looking inside, trying to pass the ball to Duncan, who by now was one of the most dominant players in the league in only his second season. The Knicks were too smart to leave him alone, so the ball ended up in the hands of Avery Johnson, one of the smallest players on the court.

An eleven-year veteran who was playing for his fifth team, Johnson sailed an eighteen-foot baseline jumper right through the rim, finding nothing but net to give San Antonio a 78–77 lead. When New York's Latrell Sprewell, who was surrounded by Duncan and Robinson, was unable to hit a last-second shot from under the basket, the Spurs ran onto the Garden floor as NBA champions.

One of the players celebrating was Duncan, sporting a gigantic smile and hugging his teammates, a somewhat emotional outburst for the usually stoic young man. He didn't care that he didn't get the final shot; all he cared about was the first-ever title the Spurs just won.

"This is a great feeling right now," Duncan said after the game. "We had such a team effort out there. Avery Johnson hits that last shot. That shows how unselfish we are, just moving the ball around the horn and getting it to the open guy."[1]

Duncan was also happy that he got to see his good friend Robinson win his first NBA title. While considered one of the best players for nearly a decade, the knock on Robinson in the media was he couldn't win

PRIME-TIME PLAYER

A sign of a great player is how well he performs in the postseason. Duncan has proven to be one of the best playoff performers ever. Among active players, he ranks seventh in playoff scoring average at 23.8 points per game, second in playoff rebounds with 1,362, second in blocks with 293, and third in points scored with 2,502.

Duncan shoots in Game 5 of the 1999 NBA Finals.

a title. With Duncan's help, that all changed in 1999.

"One of the things I remember most is [Robinson's] reaction," Duncan said. "It meant so much to him. He had worked so many years, and that was the first time he had gotten [an NBA title]. He talked about how it was the best feeling he had ever had on a team, looking around at all the people he knew he could count on, people who only cared about winning. Everybody contributed that year. Everyone trusted each other. It was great to be a part of that."[2]

MOST VALUABLE PLAYER

While Johnson hit the game-winning shot, Duncan was the reason why the Spurs won Game 5 and the championship. Duncan was named the Finals' Most Valuable Player. He dominated the Knicks by averaging 27.4 points, 14 rebounds, 2.2 blocks, and 2.4 assists in the Finals. At 23, Duncan became the second-youngest person to be named the NBA Finals' MVP.

During one stretch of Game 5, the contest was basically an old-fashioned game of one-on-one between Sprewell and Duncan. For nearly six

KNIFE COLLECTOR

While Duncan is afraid of sharks and heights, he is not afraid of sharp objects. Duncan has a large knife collection that includes a one-meter (three-foot) samurai sword.

minutes, spanning the end of the third quarter and the start of the fourth quarter, the duo combined to score 28 of the 29 points scored by the two teams.

Sprewell scored 14 consecutive points for the Knicks, often on spectacular end-to-end drives or bombs from behind the three-point line. Nearly every play had a certain flair to it. Duncan, meanwhile, scored 14 of the Spurs' 15 points. Fittingly, Duncan's points came from all over the court, methodically placing an emphasis on substance over style.

Duncan featured his now famous bank shot, hitting one from thirteen feet and then another from seven. With his back to the basket, Duncan was not to be stopped either, as he hit a baseline turnaround jumper. He then threw in a spin move that left Knicks defenders grabbing air and added a hook shot from twelve feet. The display was vintage Duncan.

"But man, when you've got a seven-footer shooting eighteen-foot bank shots—that's amazing."

—Spurs guard Mario Elie

Teammates of Duncan had seen him dominate games all season, but they were still amazed at what their seven-foot power forward could do on the court. "[Sprewell] just was rolling tonight," Spurs guard Mario Elie said after the game. "But man, when you've got a seven-footer shooting eighteen-foot bank shots—that's amazing."[3]

Duncan's scoring was vital to San Antonio's success, but his defense was a key reason the Spurs walked away with the title. With Duncan and Robinson dominating the paint and controlling the boards, the Knicks failed to score more than 89 points in any of the five games. Three times they failed to even score 80 points; they were held to 77 points in Game 1 and 67 points in Game 2 as Robinson had 5 blocks and Duncan added 4.

After losing Game 3 to the Knicks, the Spurs were able to rebound and win Game 4, 96–89. Duncan was again a force, scoring 28 points and hauling in 18 rebounds. He and Robinson also combined to block 7 shots, frustrating the Knicks anytime they tried to make a shot in the lane. In Game 5, the Spurs held New York scoreless for the final 3:12 of the game.

TIM DUNCAN'S 1999 FINALS PERFORMANCE AGAINST NEW YORK

GAME	POINTS	REBOUNDS	WINNER
Game 1	33	16	Spurs: 89–77
Game 2	25	15	Spurs: 80–67
Game 3	20	12	Knicks: 89–81
Game 4	28	18	Spurs: 96–89
Game 5	31	9	Spurs: 78–77

Larry Johnson is defended by Duncan and Sean Elliott.

"Size does matter in this league," said Knicks head coach Jeff Van Gundy, "particularly in the play-offs. And their [Duncan's and Robinson's] size beat our speed and quickness because not only did that affect us on the boards and in the post, but every penetration was a difficult, difficult shot because of their shotblocking."[4]

A WINNING COMBINATION

Since joining the Spurs in 1989 after his commitment to the Navy was over, Robinson was the heart and soul of the team. The franchise had not recorded a winning season in the six seasons prior to Robinson's arrival, bottoming out at 21–61 in 1988–89. During Robinson's rookie season, the Spurs improved to 56–26, starting a string of seven consecutive seasons of forty-seven or more wins.

Robinson was the leader on the team, and in 1999, there was nothing more his teammates wanted to do than win a title for "The Admiral." Robinson was instrumental in helping the Spurs win the title, averaging 15.8 points, 10 rebounds, 2.1 assists, and 2.4 blocked shots during the regular season. In the playoffs, Robinson scored 15.6 points per game while averaging 9.9 rebounds, 2.5 assists, and 2.4 rebounds.

But while Robinson may have still been the spiritual leader, the heart and soul of the Spurs, Duncan provided the muscle. Without Duncan, the Spurs would not have won their first title. During the regular season, Duncan scored 21.7 points and grabbed 11.4 rebounds per game while also dishing out 2.4 assists and blocking 2.5 shots per contest.

In the postseason against the best teams in the NBA, Duncan was even better than he was during the regular season. He averaged 23.2 points, 11.5 rebounds, 2.8 assists, and 2.6 blocked shots in seventeen games.

Because of his lack of flair and his desire to just play the game and not show off, many fans outside of San Antonio didn't know how good Duncan was. It was Karl Malone of Utah, not Duncan, who won the

BORING, BUT A WINNER

After a dominating performance in the 1999 postseason, especially against the New York Knicks in the Finals, Tim Duncan was named the NBA Finals' MVP. Accolades were showered on Duncan. But he also gained the tag of "boring." An article by CNNSI.com even used the word "boring" in a headline to describe Duncan. The seven-foot power forward doesn't thump his chest after impressive plays or stick out his tongue while dunking. While he does have tattoos, he doesn't wear flashy jewelry and, if possible, is happy not talking to the press. "I don't think there are words to describe Tim Duncan," teammate Sean Elliott said. "He's not flashy, he's not in your face, he doesn't have to intimidate people. He just goes out and plays the game with a lot of style, a lot of class." So while the media labels Duncan as boring, it should really label him as a winner. The 1999 title was the first of three Duncan has now won with the Spurs, and that is all that matters to him.

regular season MVP award. The 1999 postseason was a chance for Duncan to shine and show the country that he was the new leader of the Spurs.

"He's obviously the MVP of the league this year," Sean Elliott said. "You guys who didn't vote for him should be ashamed of yourself."[5]

A SHORT SEASON

Duncan and the rest of the Spurs nearly didn't get the chance to celebrate a championship. As the season was set to start in October, the players and owners were in the midst of a nasty labor dispute. Each side wanted changes in how to divide up the huge amount of money the league was making.

The players threatened to go on strike, but they didn't get the chance as the owners issued a lockout. The players were not allowed to practice or work out in NBA arenas. In fact, they couldn't even talk with their own coaches.

After experiencing success in the 1998 playoffs, the Spurs expected to compete for a title in 1999 and were looking forward to the 1998–99 season. But as

> "He's obviously the MVP of the league this year. You guys who didn't vote for him should be ashamed of yourself."
>
> —Sean Elliott

the lockout went into November and then December, there was a chance Duncan, Robinson, and the rest of the Spurs wouldn't even get to play.

As the new year started, the lockout finally came to an end, and a shortened season was scheduled to begin in February. But if the Spurs were going to win, they were going to have to be in shape, because the league scheduled a fifty-game season that was to be played in only ninety-one days.

Not surprisingly, Duncan was in top shape when the season finally tipped off. However, the Spurs started slowly, going 6–8 to start the season. But thanks to Duncan, San Antonio finished the year with a 31–5 spurt and finished 37–13, tying Utah for the best record in the league.

With Duncan leading the way, the Spurs went on one of the most impressive postseason runs in NBA history, going 15–2 in the playoffs. San Antonio's only losses were to Minnesota in the first round of the playoffs and to New York in Game 3 of the Finals. In between the two defeats were twelve consecutive wins. Including the playoffs, the Spurs won forty-six of their final fifty-three games.

THE OLYMPICS CALL

Duncan was exhausted after the season. Who wouldn't be, after playing sixty-seven games in just under five months? But with the 2000 Summer Olympics just around the corner, Team USA needed his services.

Rest is what Duncan wanted, but he had made a promise to play for Team USA. Only two weeks after winning a title with the Spurs, he was wearing

MISSING THE GAMES

Duncan helped Team USA secure a spot in the 2000 Summer Olympics by playing in the 1999 qualifying tournament. However, Duncan was unable to play in the Olympics due to a knee injury.

the red, white, and blue of Team USA in San Juan, Puerto Rico. Composed of a cast of all-stars, the United States blew through the qualifying round, securing a spot in the Olympic games to be held in Sydney, Australia, the following year.

While Duncan was doing all he could on the court for either San Antonio or the United States, he was starting to be more involved in the community off the court. Duncan has always been generous. Since coming to San Antonio, he has been involved in raising money for children's shelters.

After the Spurs won their first title, a cereal, Slam Duncans™, was produced and sold in area supermarkets. A portion of the proceeds went to several charities of Duncan's choice, including the Children's Shelter of San Antonio. Duncan was happy to help those who were less fortunate than he was.

Soon, he would take his charity to a whole new level.

CHAPTER EIGHT

Riding a Roller Coaster in 2000 and 2001

Since joining the NBA as a rookie in 1997, Duncan experienced growth on the court, going from Rookie of the Year to NBA champion. But he was also growing as a person off the court.

Duncan has always been a charitable person, hoping that he can use his power as a professional athlete to make a difference in the community. Duncan has raised money for a variety of different organizations, but especially for breast cancer, which claimed his mother's life. Since January of 2000, the Tim Duncan Bowling for Dollar$ Charity Bowl-a-thon has raised more than $650,000 for breast and prostate cancer

detection, preven-
tion, and treatment.

The proceeds
from the bowl-a-thon
helped Duncan donate
$142,000 to the San
Antonio branch of the
American Cancer
Society to help aid
breast and prostate can-

FUNDRAISERS

The Tim Duncan Foundation
holds two major fundraisers per
year. In addition to the Bowling
for Dollar$ Charity Bowl-a-thon,
the foundation also hosts the
Slam Duncan Charity Golf
Classic.

cer research. He has also given $85,000 to the San
Antonio Metropolitan Health District.

In May of 2000, Duncan hosted a "Beat Cancer"
promotion that enabled the Cancer Therapy and
Research Center to receive a $50,000 contribution.

A NEW PARTNERSHIP

In 2001, a dramatic change occurred in Duncan's life
and his charitable giving, however. Since his college
days at Wake Forest, Duncan had been dating Amy
Sherrill. Amy was with Duncan when he was named
Rookie of the Year and won his first title with the
Spurs. She was there when he first re-signed with the
Spurs during the summer of 2000.

In the summer, Duncan married his longtime
girlfriend, and together they have brought happiness
to thousands of children in the San Antonio area.
Before the end of the year, the couple created the

Duncan shares a laugh with his girlfriend, Amy Sherrill, during a 2000 news conference announcing his intent to stay with the Spurs.

Tim Duncan Foundation, in which Amy serves as the executive vice president. The Tim Duncan Foundation is designed to encourage "the areas of health awareness and research, education and youth sports and recreation" in San Antonio, Winston-Salem, and the Virgin Islands.

"This is very exciting for me," said Duncan. "I've been involved in the community, but now through my Foundation, I can support worthwhile causes not only in San Antonio, but also in North Carolina where I went to college, and back home in the U.S. Virgin Islands. All of these places are very special to me, and I feel blessed that I can help make a difference to the people in these communities."[1]

"Amy helped give more direction to Tim's already good intentions," said Lon Babby, Duncan's agent. "She helped take everything to a new level."[2]

GETTING RESULTS

It didn't take long for the Tim Duncan Foundation to start producing results. The couple soon introduced the Tim Duncan's Character Program, an educational incentive program that each year rewards 3,000 Bexar County (where San Antonio is located) students who show outstanding character traits and also make good choices. The program includes students in kindergarten through twelfth grade.

GOOD DEEDS

In addition to the charities Duncan supports through the Tim Duncan Foundation, the Spurs' power forward also supports the Children's Bereavement Center, the Children's Center of San Antonio, and the Cancer Therapy and Research Center.

> **"The best way to describe this program is that we wanted to find a way to reward students for doing good things and making good choices."**
>
> **—Tim Duncan**

The six character traits the program is based on are integrity, respect, dependability, fairness, caring, and civic responsibility. Some of the rewards given to students include tickets to Spurs games, Character Program t-shirts, passes to Sea World, and achievement certificates.

"The best way to describe this program is that we wanted to find a way to reward students for doing good things and making good choices," Duncan said. "All of the qualities that go into being a good person. Things like respect, integrity, and being part of your community are traits that we all need to practice. We think by recognizing those who have these values we can encourage more and more students to actively think about demonstrating strong character on a daily basis."[3]

On Duncan's Web site, Slamduncan.com, he answers a series of questions from fans who write in. A grandmother was ecstatic that her granddaughter was nominated and won for the Character Award program, and she wrote to thank Duncan. She wanted to know just what helped Duncan decide to start his Character Program. The answer centered on the nursery rhyme his mother used to recite—*Good, Better, Best. Never let it rest, Until your Good is Better, and your Better is your Best.*

"GOOD GUY"

The Sporting News named Duncan one of the "Good Guys" in sports in both 2001 and 2002.

"I guess it just stuck," Duncan wrote, "and when my wife and I wanted to start a powerful community program, we knew passing along the importance of hard work and good character to the children was a perfect fit. We believe that it is our duty to give back to our community and thought a character program was perfect to give the kids today the tools to succeed in life."[4]

During his life, Duncan has earned numerous awards. But Duncan probably is just as proud of a community

KEEPING KIDS OFF DRUGS

Duncan is also involved with the San Antonio Drug Free Kids League. Coaches are asked to come in and teach children basketball skills, which has helped get children off the streets and give them goals to achieve and a sense of accomplishment.

Duncan helps a student during an after-school program.

service award he received as he is of his NBA Finals MVP awards. In 2001, the NBA acknowledged Duncan's hard work in the community by awarding him the Home Team Community Service Award.

Winning of the award allowed Duncan to name a charity to receive $25,000. He selected the San Antonio's Children's Shelter, the largest and oldest shelter for abused, abandoned, and neglected children in Bexar County.

Since its inception, the Tim Duncan Foundation has raised more than $700,000 for breast and prostate cancer prevention, detection, treatment, and research programs. The Sixth Annual Bowling for Dollar$ event raised $135,000. With additional funds from the Tim Duncan Foundation, a grant of $200,000 was awarded to the Cancer Therapy and Research Center located in San Antonio, allowing for prevention, detection, and treatment services to underserved and uninsured people in and around the Bexar County area.

PROVING HIS LOVE

The union of Duncan and his wife almost never happened. When Duncan graduated from Wake Forest, Amy figured her relationship with Duncan was over. She had heard the stories about NBA players who have girlfriends in nearly every city in which their teams play. She did not want to be involved with that kind of life.

Duncan, however, made sure Amy knew how much he cared for her. During his rookie season, he called her every day, sometimes many times each day.

While Duncan is somewhat shy when it comes to talking about his relationship with his wife, she said those calls proved just how much Duncan cared for her. "I was still in college, and we had those first couple of months when I was convinced you [Duncan] were going to go off and do bad things," Amy said to Duncan. "Then all the uncertainties went away, and you did that for me, by calling and reassuring me that . . . you weren't out there doing bad things. You rekindled that belief."[5]

Duncan has always been able to joke with friends and have fun. But something about being with Amy makes him a more complete person, and it is easy to see that Duncan has complete trust in his wife. Those who spend time with the couple know it is a union that will last for years to come.

"It's not a typical NBA relationship," said Babby, Duncan's agent. "It's a real marriage, a real partnership. You have no doubt they're going to be together in thirty years."[6]

> **"It's not a typical NBA relationship. It's a real marriage, a real partnership."**
>
> **—Duncan's agent, Lon Babby**

FACING CHALLENGES

Duncan needed a great year personally in 2001, because 2000 did not end the way Duncan would have wanted. Coming off the title in 1999, the Spurs were expected to contend for the 2000 NBA title as well. When the season started, however, a key player was out of the lineup.

Small forward Sean Elliott, who was instrumental in the team's title run in 1999, was unable to play while recovering from a kidney transplant. With Elliott out of the lineup, Duncan had to do even more for the Spurs, including seeing time at small forward, where he had to face the basket more than he was used to doing.

Undaunted, Duncan took to the challenge. Playing with his back to the basket from his power forward position, Duncan continued to dominate any defender guarding him, whether by hitting his now-famous bank shot or a combination of hook shots and short jumpers.

When asked to slide over to small forward during the game, Duncan squared up and faced the basket. It was much like his days as a point guard during his first years in high school, when he applied the drills taught to him by his brother-in-law. While he may be seven feet tall now, Duncan is still one of the quickest players in the league, and he uses that speed to drive around defenders to the basket or back in toward the goal and post up if he is guarded by a smaller defender.

Duncan was named to the All-Star team once again and came away with the game's MVP award by scoring 24 points and grabbing 14 rebounds for the West squad. With Duncan and Robinson anchoring the defense, the Spurs were allowing only 90.2 points per game while limiting opponents to less than 43 percent shooting from the field.

After seventy-four games, Duncan was having his best season yet, averaging 23.2 points and 12.4 rebounds, both career highs. He also set new career highs with 234 assists (3.2 per game) and 66 steals. The Spurs were heading for the postseason and a fifty-three-win season.

DEALING WITH AN INJURY

But Duncan, and the Spurs as well, suffered a devastating blow on April 11. During the middle of a game, Duncan's knee made a sudden turn in the wrong direction. Immediately, Duncan knew something was wrong and soon found out he suffered torn cartilage in his knee.

With the playoffs rapidly approaching, it was the worst time for Duncan to suffer an injury, much less a knee injury. The Spurs played their final four games with Duncan watching from the bench. They entered the postseason as the fourth seed in the Western

Duncan is double-teamed by the Cleveland Cavaliers' Michael Hawkins and Chris Gatling at the Alamodome.

Conference. The team's first-round matchup was against the Phoenix Suns, and the big question on everyone's mind was if Duncan would be able to play.

That question was answered before Game 1 ever started. Duncan was ruled out. With their star power forward watching from the bench in a suit, the Spurs fell to the Suns, 72–70. So, would Duncan be able to play in Game 2?

"I'm not very good at predicting the future, but he's rehabbing every day and he improves X percent every day," Popovich, the Spurs' coach, said before Game 2. "When he's able to go out on the court and perform without danger of injury and he can help our team, then we'll have him out on the court."[7]

When Game 2 was set to start and the teams took

STAYING IN SAN ANTONIO

During the summer of 2000, Tim Duncan had a huge decision to make—stay in San Antonio or leave for another NBA city and a huge contract. Duncan was a free agent and had to decide what he wanted to do. The Orlando Magic tried hard to get Duncan, already considered one of the best players in the league, to sign with the team. During a visit to Orlando, Duncan was treated by the Magic to the finest the city had to offer. That made Duncan's decision to stay in San Antonio or head to Orlando a tough one. The city of San Antonio went to great lengths to keep Duncan in the Alamo City. Billboards and posters were plastered around town saying "Stay Tim Stay." David Robinson cut his vacation to Hawaii short to visit with Duncan. In the end, Duncan remained a Spur. He cited, among other things, his desire to win another title with his good friend Robinson. He accomplished that goal in 2003.

the court, San Antonio fans were hoping to see No. 21 in action. Again, however, Duncan was unable to go. Still, the Spurs rallied to win and even the series at one game apiece.

In the end, the Suns would win the series in four games. Duncan never was able to take the court for the Spurs. It brought a disappointing end to what was at one time a promising season.

DIFFICULT CHOICES

Duncan then faced another disappointment. After helping the United States qualify for the 2000 Summer Olympics in 1999, Duncan was looking forward to going to Sydney and playing for Team USA. Duncan underwent knee surgery on May 24 to repair the torn cartilage in his knee and did not start full rehabilitation until two weeks before the start of the Games.

Duncan was torn, because he wanted to keep his commitment with Team USA. At the same time, he didn't want to suffer any setback that would affect his upcoming season with the Spurs. In addition, Duncan's father was suffering from a number of illnesses. Duncan did not want to be away from his ill father for too long. In the end, Duncan decided being with his father and resting for the start of the regular season was more important than fulfilling a lifelong dream of competing in the Olympics.

9

Sorrow and Joy

CHAPTER NINE

In 2000, Duncan suffered through the disappointment of suffering a knee injury, watching the Spurs lose in the playoffs, and then having to withdraw from the 2000 Olympic basketball team.

Duncan was able to put those tough times behind him the following year as he got married to his long-time girlfriend. Together, they created the Tim Duncan Foundation, allowing the San Antonio area to experience the charitable side of Duncan.

In 2002, Duncan would experience the ultimate joy as a basketball player on a personal level. However, his ability to celebrate the top personal award in the NBA came only after suffering through deep sorrow. Since the death of Duncan's mother, Ione, the day before his fourteenth birthday, Duncan had come to rely on his father, William. Name an important event in Duncan's life, and his father was there to witness it.

As Duncan began to blossom as a basketball player in high school, his father was there, helping his son handle the sudden interest of college coaches. During Duncan's magnificent college career at Wake Forest, William could often be seen in the stands, cheering for his son and the rest of the Demon Deacons.

Graduation came, and sitting in the audience was a proud William Duncan as he watched his son receive his diploma and keep the promise made to his late wife. Four years after Duncan graduated from Wake Forest, the university retired his No. 21 uniform. Both Duncan and his father were on hand to witness the occasion.

Then came the Rookie of the Year award in 1998 and the NBA title the Spurs won in 1999. There to celebrate with Duncan was his father. But as time passed, William was unable to be with his son as much. William suffered through a series of illnesses. In the summer of 2000, part of the reason Duncan chose to skip the Summer Olympics was because he wanted to spend time with his father.

TRUE LEADER

In 2001–02, Duncan led the Spurs in scoring seventy-two times and was the team's top rebounder in a game sixty-nine times. He also made nearly 80 percent of his free throws after making only 62 percent of his attempts the previous season.

After a fantastic regular season in 2002, in which San Antonio won fifty-eight games, Duncan and the Spurs entered the playoffs with the second-best record in the Western Conference. Through the first three games of the best-of-five series, the Spurs held a 2–1 advantage.

CONSISTENCY

In his first eight **NBA seasons**, Duncan averaged at least 20 points and 11 rebounds in each of his first eight NBA seasons. For his career, Duncan has averaged 22.1 points, 12 rebounds 3.1 assists, and 2.5 blocks per game.

A TRAGIC LOSS

Duncan then faced tragedy for the second time in his life. On a Monday morning in late April, Duncan was told his father was hospitalized. Without hesitation, Duncan left for North Carolina. Later that day, William, 71, died of prostate cancer. Duncan remained with his family and did not play in Game 4.

Even opposing coaches and players were affected by Duncan's circumstances. Seattle SuperSonics coach Nate McMillan said it was tough to see Duncan lose his father. Several of the Seattle players were affected by the passing of William Duncan as well. During the summer of 1999, when Team USA was training in Puerto Rico, Duncan had his father come to the island and meet his teammates. By being with

William, a lot of the players understood why Duncan was such a gentleman both on and off the court.

"It really makes it hard," said Seattle forward Vin Baker, who sponsored Duncan during a recruiting visit to the University of Hartford. "I just really feel for his family right now. It's such a devastating thing to happen to such a good person and at such a pivotal time in the season."[1]

Baker's teammate Gary Payton was also affected by the news of William Duncan's death and expressed the sadness he felt for Duncan.

"We hung around in Puerto Rico," said Payton. "His dad was sick during that time and everyone knew it. We thought he was getting better. I just asked him [Duncan] about his father when we were in San Antonio, and he had said he was OK. So it was really a shock to me.

"I just hope that everything is going to be all right with his family and that he'll be back to play and that this will not be on his mind too much."[2]

SHOWING HIS STRENGTH

Without Duncan in the lineup for Game 4 and with center David Robinson ailing due to a bad back, the Spurs lost to the Sonics, setting up a do-or-die Game 5. With the season on the line and Robinson unable to play, San Antonio needed their star power forward more than ever.

The day before the fifth game, the Spurs learned Duncan would be back in time to play. But how well could he play one day after burying his father? Would he be able to concentrate on the game, or would his emotions affect his play?

When the Spurs took the court for the tip-off, Duncan was standing alongside his teammates, ready to face the Sonics. The cheers from the San Antonio faithful for Duncan and his return shook the building.

Carried by the support of the crowd, Duncan turned in an amazing, even legendary, performance. Within minutes, any doubts about him being able to concentrate on the game were dashed as he scored 6 of the first 8 San Antonio points. By the end of the game, Duncan had 23 points, 9 rebounds, and 7 blocks, leading the Spurs to a 101–78 victory and a berth in the second round of the playoffs against the Los Angeles Lakers. After the game, Duncan said he was glad to be back wearing the uniform of the Spurs.

"It's been a whirlwind," Duncan said. "It's great to be back. ... It's a sanctuary out there [on the court]. It's basketball, and you get away from everything else."[3]

The performance by Duncan was a jaw-dropping spectacle, at least to those outside of the team's locker room. Members of the team said Duncan was just doing what was expected of him.

"That's what superstars do for a team," said

Duncan goes up for a shot against the Lakers in Game 1.

STAYING IN SAN ANTONIO

Duncan lives up to the old saying "the cream rises to the top." Entering the 2005–06 season, Duncan had played in 105 career playoff games and performed better in the postseason than the regular season. His 23.8 points, 13.0 rebounds, 3.6 assists, and 2.8 blocks per game are all better than his regular-season career averages. He has scored in double-figures in 103 of his 105 postseason games and has recorded 9 20-rebound games and 3 triple-doubles.

Popovich. "They make so many different things happen at both ends of the floor."[4]

A CONSISTENT PERFORMER

Duncan was at his best nearly every night during the 2001-02 season. Facing in-state rival Houston in December, Duncan led a 10–2 spurt late in the game to lift the Spurs to an 85–75 win. For the night, Duncan had 25 points, 12 rebounds, 4 blocked shots, 4 steals, and 3 assists.

For Duncan, that was just an average game. During the season, he set new career highs in scoring (25.5 points per game) and rebounding (12.7 per game). In the team's seventy-ninth game of the year, Duncan was nearly perfect against the Grizzlies.

Mr. Automatic hit 12 of his 17 shots, including his only three-point attempt, and was 5-for-5 from the free-throw line to score 30 points in a 113–92 victory. Duncan was also busy blocking out his opponents in the paint, grabbing 14 rebounds. His court vision was on full display, as he dished out 7 assists and blocked 4 shots while coming away with 2 steals.

Duncan finished fifth in the league in scoring, second in rebounding, and third in blocked shots (2.48 average). His 67 double-doubles was tops in the league. He was named the Western Conference's player of the week five times during the regular season and the conference's player of the month in December, March, and April.

A HUMBLE MVP

It was the best season of his career. Still, Duncan was locked in a battle with several other NBA stars for the Most Valuable Player award. Jason Kidd of the New Jersey Nets was having an outstanding season, as was Tracy McGrady of Orlando, and Shaquille O'Neal of the Lakers.

In 2001, Duncan finished second to Allen Iverson of Philadelphia for the MVP award. The

CLOSE RACE

Duncan's fifty-seven-point margin of victory for the MVP award over Jason Kidd of the New Jersey Nets was the smallest since Karl Malone of Utah edged Alonzo Mourning by fifty-four points in 1999.

Duncan was named MVP two years in a row.

Maurice Podoloff Trophy
2002-03 NBA Most Valuable Player
TIM DUNCAN
San Antonio Spurs

result would be different this time, however. Barely one week after the death of his father, Duncan learned he was named the league's 2001–02 MVP, narrowly edging out Kidd for the honor.

Duncan said his goal entering the season was to have his best year as a professional, and he was certainly able to cross that goal off his list. But in typical Duncan fashion, he said there were several other players deserving of the MVP trophy as well.

"I'm not going to give it back, but if someone else won it, I wouldn't dispute it," Duncan said. "[The award] was kind of a goal I had in mind. It puts a top on the season that we had."[5]

The Spurs had a remarkable regular season, but the Lakers ended San Antonio's title hopes for the second straight year by claiming a 4–1 series victory in the second round. But Duncan would come back in 2003, winning his second consecutive MVP award and leading the Spurs to their second title in Robinson's final season.

Though he was the team's best player, Duncan and the Spurs' championships were linked to Robinson. With Robinson's retirement after the 2003 Finals, the Spurs were, without a doubt, now Duncan's team.

He would not disappoint.

CHAPTER TEN

Olympic Disappointment Leads to Championship Celebration

In leading the Spurs to titles in 1999 and 2003, Duncan proved he was a winner. But those titles were won when David Robinson was still with the team. Until the Spurs won a title without Robinson, critics would continue to say Duncan couldn't win without having Robinson by his side.

It was time to quiet the critics in 2005. With Duncan leading the way, the Spurs won fifty-nine games, topping fifty wins in a season for the sixth consecutive year. In the playoffs, when the Spurs needed him most, Duncan came through for his team—just as he always has.

As the second seed in the Western Conference, the Spurs disposed of seventh-seeded Denver four games to one. Then came a 4–2 series victory against Seattle in the second round. In the Western Conference Finals, the Spurs recorded an impressive 4–1 series win against top-seeded and high-scoring Phoenix, led by league MVP Steve Nash.

After struggling from the free-throw line and missing a dunk in Game 4, which Phoenix won to avoid a sweep, Duncan was his usual masterful self in Game 5, scoring 31 points and grabbing 15 rebounds in a 101–95 Spurs win.

"Tim Duncan was a possessed individual," Popovich said. "You would never know it by looking at his face or talking to him. What he did tonight, he's done many, many times. It's just who he is. It's what makes him so special."[1]

With the win in Game 5, the Spurs earned a date in the Finals against defending champion Detroit Pistons, the only team other than San Antonio or the Los Angeles Lakers to win an NBA title since 1999.

FATHER TIM

After winning his third NBA title in 2005, Duncan and his wife, Amy, became first-time parents when they welcomed a daughter into the world.

A LEADER IN THE FINALS

Everyone—players, coaches, fans, and the media— was expecting a grueling series. Everyone was right, though it looked as if the Spurs were going to run away with the title as they won Game 1 by 15 points and Game 2 by 21 points.

But the Pistons were not going to go down easy, especially when the series headed to Detroit. Behind a suffocating defense, the Pistons won Game 3, 96–79, and then won Game 4 by 31 points.

Then came the pivotal Game 5, a thriller that would go into overtime, though it nearly didn't. Duncan ended the game with 26 points and 19 rebounds. But he missed 6 of 7 free throws during the fourth quarter and was unable to tip the ball in at the buzzer, a basket that would have given the Spurs a win in regulation. The fourth quarter was a spurt Duncan described as an absolute nightmare. However, Robert Horry came through for the Spurs by hitting a three-pointer with 5.8 seconds remaining in the extra period to give his team a 96–95 win and a 3–2 lead in the series against the Pistons.

The Pistons came back to win Game 6 as Duncan struggled against the Detroit defense, setting up the all-or-nothing Game 7. With the spotlight at its brightest on the league's biggest stage, it was time for Duncan to come through once again. In Game 7, Duncan was at his best, leading the Spurs to an 81–74

Duncan battles for the ball with Detroit's Rasheed Wallace.

FOLLOWING MICHAEL

By winning the Finals' MVP award in 2005, Duncan became just the second player to win the honor in each of his first three trips to the Finals. Only Michael Jordan, who won six Finals MVP awards in six tries, is in that exclusive club.

victory and cutting that link to Robinson, who believes his former teammate has nothing left to prove.

"I would hope in everybody's mind that Tim Duncan doesn't have to do anything to validate his career," Robinson said during an interview on Sporting News Radio. "You know how the world loves to raise that bar up higher and higher and make you jump a little bit higher? But Tim Duncan, in my mind, he's the man. He's one of the best players in NBA history."[2]

Like a skilled surgeon, Duncan, who was named the NBA Finals' MVP for the third time, cut apart the Detroit defense to score 25 points and grab 11 rebounds. During any Spurs run, Duncan was right in the middle of it, either by hitting his shot, making a key pass for an assist, grabbing an offensive rebound to keep the possession alive, or diving on the floor after loose balls.

"It wasn't the greatest of games but there was a stretch where I felt really good and I just wanted to be assertive at that point," said Duncan, who actually hit only 10 of his 27 shots. "They just kept coming to me and kept giving me the opportunities and I got one to fall in and two to fall in and things started happening. Then I was able to draw some double-teams and got some guys some open shots."[3]

The two teams were tied 57–57 heading into the fourth quarter. But the final twelve minutes belonged to Duncan. He started the quarter with power, slamming home a dunk to snap the deadlock. With the Spurs holding a 64–61 lead, Duncan raced to grab a missed three-pointer by Horry. The Pistons quickly doubled him with two defenders, and Duncan fired a pass to Bruce Bowen. The veteran calmly hit a three-pointer to give the Spurs a six-point lead.

A LITTLE OFF THE TOP
Duncan went more than six months without a haircut in 2005. Before getting a haircut, days after Christmas, Duncan had not gotten a haircut since before the 2005 NBA Finals series against Detroit.

Later in the quarter, Duncan again hustled to a loose ball and called timeout before going out of bounds. When play resumed, the ball ended up in his hands. Before the Detroit defenders were able to close in on him, Duncan sank a twenty-foot jumper to make it a 69–63 Spurs lead. Then came a pass out of a double-team to Manu Ginobili for a three-pointer. That basket gave the Spurs the momentum they needed to hold off the Pistons down the stretch.

"His complete game is so sound, so fundamental, so unnoticed at times, because if he didn't score, people think, 'Well, he didn't do anything,'" Popovich said. "But he was incredible and he was the force that got it done for us."[4]

The fourth quarter, however, wasn't even Duncan's best quarter. The Pistons built a nine-point lead and looked poised to take control of the game. But Duncan, who missed his first seven shots of the second half, would not allow it. Doing everything but wearing a Superman cape, Duncan put the Spurs on his back and carried the team to a 57–55 lead, putting them back into the game.

Duncan scored 12 points in the third quarter, including nine over the final 4:01 of the quarter. Duncan hit a pair of free throws to cut the Detroit lead to four points. Thirty-one seconds later, he was fouled while hitting his shot. Duncan completed the three-point play with a free throw to pull the Spurs to within one point, at 52–51.

Duncan then tied the game at 53–53 with 2:56 left in the quarter on a short bank shot and then hit a jumper with 52 seconds remaining to push San Antonio ahead by two, 57–55. "We only go as far as Tim takes us," Horry said. "And today he took us to the top."[5]

Duncan goes up for a rebound with the Pistons' Ben Wallace.

AN OLYMPIAN

The NBA title quickly made everyone forget the troubles Duncan had during the 2004 Summer Olympics in Athens, Greece. After withdrawing from the 2000 Olympic team due to a knee injury and his father's health, Duncan was finally going to fulfill a lifelong dream of participating in the Games and duplicate his sister Tricia's feat of competing in the Olympics.

Duncan's reputation as a winner and leader preceded him now, and in July, he and Allen Iverson were unanimously selected as co-captains of the team by the rest of the Team USA squad. Coach Larry Brown was highly in favor of the vote, saying that both Duncan and Iverson were the perfect choices to lead a relatively young team.

> **"His complete game is so sound, so fundamental, so unnoticed at times, because if he didn't score, people think, 'Well, he didn't do anything.' But he was incredible and he was the force that got it done for us."**
>
> **— Spurs head coach Gregg Popovich**

Just being an Olympian was a dream come true, so Duncan was humbled by his selection as a team captain. "It's an honor to be on the Olympic team, period. And, then, to be put in a captain spot on this team is a big responsibility but it is one that is shouldered by a lot of different guys," said Duncan. He led Team USA to a 10–0 record during the Olympic qualifying tournament in Puerto Rico by averaging 15.6 points and 8.0 rebounds. "I feel comfortable, being one of the elders, so I will try to do my best. With Allen and myself, we bring two distinctive ways of doing things, but we bring two ways that are good for the team. That's to go out, play hard and get the job done."[6]

Duncan performed well in Athens, but the excitement of playing in the Olympics quickly turned to disappointment. Team USA struggled to find the winning team chemistry, and it showed on the court. Despite scoring 15 points and grabbing 16 rebounds in the first game of the tournament, Duncan and the United States were walloped by Puerto Rico, 92–73.

The U.S. rallied to beat Greece and Australia as Duncan averaged 16 points and 10 rebounds in those two games. But Duncan probably could have done more if not for constant foul trouble. Playing his usual style of basketball, Duncan was called for fouls he never gets whistled for in the NBA.

As the tournament went on, Duncan's frustration mounted as he continuously found himself in foul trouble, often called for nit-picky fouls. With Duncan having to spend more time on the bench than planned, the team struggled without their one true big-man on the court.

In the fourth game of pool play, Lithuania handed the Americans their second loss, a 94–90 setback. When on the court, Duncan played well, scoring 16 points and grabbing 12 rebounds, the fourth straight game in which he led the team in rebounding. After two more wins, Team USA was able to qualify for the medal round and face Argentina for the right to play for the gold medal.

Once again, however, Duncan was saddled with

WHERE'S THE SUN?

As the defending NBA champion San Antonio Spurs prepared for the 2005–06 season, the club decided to train in the Virgin Islands. Duncan was more than happy to be back home and hoped to show his teammates where he grew up on nearby St. Croix. The only problem was the weather. As the team plane landed on a Saturday, all that could be seen outside the window were raindrops. The next day, St. Croix was soaked as 12.5 centimeters (5 inches) of rain fell, while St. Thomas was hit with 7.5 cm (3 in). But that did not stop anyone from having fun. Native islanders were thrilled to have Duncan back home and put banners up welcoming their hero home, leading Duncan's teammates to give their superstar a lot of good-natured ribbing.

foul problems, scoring only 10 points and grabbing 6 rebounds in 20 minutes of action before fouling out. Team USA was unable to overcome Duncan's absence on the floor and lost 89–81.

Lithuania's Ramunas Siskauskas battles for the ball with Duncan.

"Timmy was going to be a big part of what we planned to do," said Popovich, who was an assistant coach with Team USA. "We couldn't do that. He got hammered and hammered and he was afraid to touch anybody. He kept his cool when a lot of guys would have exploded."[7]

Team USA then defeated Lithuania 104–96 to claim the bronze medal. But for Duncan, the vision he had in his mind of playing in the Olympics did not live

TIM DUNCAN'S POSTSEASON STATISTICS

Year	Games	Average	Rebounds	Blocks	Assists	Steals
1998	9	20.7	81	23	17	5
1999	17	23.2	195	45	13	13
2001	13	24.4	188	35	49	14
2002	9	27.6	130	39	45	6
2003	24	24.7	369	79	127	15
2004	10	22.1	113	20	32	8
2005	23	23.6	286	52	63	8

up to reality. In what was considered an outburst by Duncan, he did not have glowing remarks about his time in Athens.

"I'm gonna say it nicely. It's not been fun," said Duncan, who was called for 34 fouls in nine games, an average of nearly 4 per game, and fouled out four times—something that is a rare occurrence in the NBA for Duncan. "I'm 95 percent sure my FIBA [international] career is over."[8]

While disappointed with the officiating and the overall experience of not winning a gold medal, Duncan was still his normal stoic self. When asked if he would tell other NBA players to avoid playing in international events such as the Olympics, he just said he would not try to share his experience with anybody.

TEAM LEADER

Duncan's international career may have come to an end, but his career with the Spurs continues to thrive. By the age of twenty-nine, Duncan had won three NBA titles. With young players such as Tony Parker and Manu Ginobili on the team, San Antonio is in great shape to continue being one of the best teams in the NBA.

But the Spurs are without question Duncan's team. He is their leader. His skill allows the Spurs to win on the court, while his humor keeps them loose and relaxed away from it. There is no telling how good Duncan can be, but most people know he is already one of the best.

"He's obviously the best player in the NBA, and not just because of his skill level," Houston Rockets coach Jeff Van Gundy said. "I think it's his maturity, his knowledge of the game, that he cares just about winning. You can just watch a guy play and know if he's truly into winning or not. That guy's truly into winning.

"So to me, not only is he the best player, but he's somebody that obviously San Antonio is going to have for a long time. I don't think it's an exaggeration to say that this league can build around Tim, because of his unselfishness, and because of what he offers as a person and as a basketball player. He's that special."[9]

CAREER STATISTICS

YEAR	TEAM	G	MIN	FGM–A	FG%	FTM–A
97–98	San Antonio	82	3,204	706–1,287	0.549	319–482
98–99	San Antonio	50	1,963	418–845	0.495	247–358
99–00	San Antonio	74	2,875	628–1,281	0.490	459–603
00–01	San Antonio	82	3,174	702–1,406	0.499	409–662
01–02	San Antonio	82	3,329	764–1,504	0.508	560–701
02–03	San Antonio	81	3,181	714–1,392	0.513	450–634
03–04	San Antonio	69	2,527	592–1,181	0.501	352–588
04–05	San Antonio	66	2,203	517–1,042	0.496	305–455
05–06	San Antonio	80	2,784	574–1,185	0.484	335–533
Career		666	25,240	5,615–11,123	0.505	3,436–5,016

KEY:
G = Games Played
MIN = Minutes Played
FGM-A = Field Goals Made-Attempted
FG% = Field Goal Percentage
FTM-A = Free Throws Made-Attempted
FT% = Free Throw Percentage
REB = Rebounds
AST = Assists
STL = Steals
BLK = Blocked Shots
PTS = Points Scored
AVG = Points Per Game Average

FT%	REB	AST	STL	BLK	PTS	AVG
0.662	977	224	55	206	1,731	21.1
0.690	571	121	45	126	1,084	21.7
0.761	918	234	66	165	1,716	23.2
0.618	997	245	70	192	1,820	22.2
0.799	1,042	307	61	203	2,089	25.5
0.710	1,043	316	55	237	1,884	23.3
0.599	859	213	62	185	1,538	22.3
0.670	732	179	45	174	1,342	20.3
0.629	881	253	70	162	1,485	18.6
0.685	8,020	2,092	529	1,650	14,689	22.1

CAREER ACHIEVEMENTS

★ Named the NBA's MVP in 2002 and 2003 (one of ten players in NBA history to win multiple MVP Awards).

★ Named the NBA Finals' MVP in 1999, 2003, and 2005.

★ Only the second player in history to earn Finals MVP honors in each of his first three trips to the Finals.

★ One of just four players to be named Finals MVP three or more times.

★ The first player in NBA history to be named to both an All-NBA Team and an All-Defensive Team in each of his first eight seasons.

★ Just the fifth player in league history to earn All-NBA First Team honors in each of his first eight seasons, joining Elgin Baylor (first ten seasons), Bob Pettit (ten), Larry Bird (nine), and Oscar Robertson (nine).

★ Has earned All-Defensive First Team honors six times and Second Team honors twice (1998 and 2004).

★ The 1998 Rookie of the Year.

★ Named the co-MVP of the 2000 All-Star Game.

★ Named the NBA Player of the Week seventeen times and the Player of the Month four times.

★ Named an All-Star seven straight seasons (no game was held in 1999).

★ Leads all players in the NBA in double-doubles over the last eight seasons with 445 double-doubles in 586 career games.

★ Entering the 2005-06 season, has scored in double-figures in 569 of his 586 career games.

★ Among Spurs all-time NBA leaders ranks fifth in games, third in points, second in rebounds, and second in blocks.

CHAPTER NOTES

CHAPTER 1. A TRUE LEADER

1. "Duncan has triple-double in clinching victory," *ESPN.com,* June 15, 2003, <http://sports.espn.go.com/nba/recap?gameId=230615024> (November 9, 2005).

2. Johnny Ludden, "The Spurs are back on top of NBA," *MySA.com,* June 16, 2003, <http://mysanantonio.com/specials/spurschamps/ stories/1012681.shtml> (November 9, 2005).

3. Ibid.

4. "Duncan has triple-double in clinching victory," *ESPN.com,* June 15, 2003, <http://sports.espn.go.com/nba/recap?gameId=230615024> (November 9, 2005).

5. Dave Glenn, "ACC in the NBA: Tim Duncan," *ACC Area Sports Journal,* May 5, 2003, <http://accsports.com/coverstory/xxvi/coverstoryxxvil8.jsp> (November 9, 2005).

6. "Duncan, Robinson share SI sportsman award," *SI.com,* December 8, 2003, <http://sportsillustrated.cnn.com/2003/basketball/nba/12/08/ bc.bkn.spurshonored.ap/> (November 10, 2005).

CHAPTER 2. GROWING UP ON ST. CROIX

1. S.L. Price, "The Quiet Man," *SI.com,* December 15, 2003, <http://premium.si.cnn.com/pr/subs/siexclusive/2003/12/08/duncan1215/ index.html> (November 14, 2005).

2. "Spur of the moment," *CNN/SI.com,* June 29, 1999, <http://cnnsi.com/basketball/nba/1999/pla…ews/1999/06/04/duncan_ stcroix/> (November 13, 2005).

3. Ibid.

CHAPTER 3. A LIFE CHANGED FOREVER

1. Chip Brown, "Tim Duncan goes from island life to life in the NBA," *Texas Sports*, October 26, 1997, <http://www.texnews.com/texsports97/duncan102697.html> (November 20, 2005).

2. S.L. Price, "The Quiet Man," *SI.com,* December 15, 2003, <http://premium.si.cnn.com/pr/subs/siexclusive/2003/12/08/duncan1215/index.html> (November 14, 2005).

3. Michael Hunt, "Dunkin' Duncan: Hurricane Hugo led star to Wake Forest," *Badger Plus Online*, March 15, 1996, <http://jsonline.com/badger/arc/0409/dunc314.html> (November 22, 2005).

CHAPTER 4. SETTLING IN AT WAKE FOREST

1. Chip Brown, "Tim Duncan goes from island life to life in the NBA," *Texas Sports,* October 26, 1997, <http://www.texnews.com/texsports97/duncan102697.html> (November 20, 2005).

2. Michael Hunt, "Dunkin' Duncan: Hurricane Hugo led star to Wake Forest," *Badger Plus Online*, March 15, 1996, <http://jsonline.com/badger/arc/0409/dunc314.html> (November 22, 2005).

3. Ibid.

CHAPTER 5. STAYING PAVES THE WAY TO NBA STARDOM

1. "21 questions with Tim Duncan," *Slamduncan.com*, <http://www.slamduncan.com/news-21questions.php> (November 14, 2005).

CHAPTER 6. ROOKIE OF THE YEAR

1. "Spurs' Duncan hoping to add another ring to dream career," *ESPN.com*, June 9, 2005, <http://sports.espn.go.com/espn/wire?section=nba&id=2080853> November 29, 2005.

2. "Duncan Named NBA's Best Rookie," *CBSnews.com*, April 27, 1998, <http://www.cbsnews.com/stories/1998/04/27/archive/main8155.shtml> (November 28, 2005).

3. Ibid.

CHAPTER 7. JUST CALL HIM CHAMP

1. "Tim-VP: CNN/SI's Vince Cellini chats with Tim Duncan after Game 5," *CNNSI.com,* June 27, 1999, <http://sportsillustrated.cnn.com/basket-ball/nba/1999/playoffs/news/1999/06/25/duncan_cellini/> (December 3, 2005).

2. Dave Glenn, "ACC in the NBA: Tim Duncan," *ACC Area Sports Journal,* May 5, 2003, <http://accsports.com/coverstory/xxvi/coverstoryxxvil8.jsp> (November 9, 2005).

3. "'Little General' Marches Spurs to First Title," *NBA.com,* June 27, 1999, <http://aol.nba.com/history/finals/19981999.html> (December 4, 2005).

4. Ibid.

5. "Duncan: A quiet, boring, dominant MVP," *CNNSI.com,* June 28, 1999, <http://sportsillustrated.cnn.com/basketball/nba/1999/playoffs/news/19 9/06/25/duncan_boring/> (December 3, 2005).

CHAPTER 8. RIDING A ROLLER COASTER IN 2000 AND 2001

1. "#21 announces the Tim Duncan Foundation," *Spurs.com,* November 2001, <http://aol.nba.com/spurs/community/21_Announces_the_Tim_Duncan_F-31744-70.html> (November 25, 2005).

2. Dave Glenn, "ACC in the NBA: Tim Duncan," *ACC Area Sports Journal,* May 5, 2003, <http://accsports.com/coverstory/xxvi/coverstoryxxvil8.jsp> (November 9, 2005).

3. "Tim Duncan's Character Program," *Slamduncan.com,* December 2001, <http://www.slamduncan.com/news-character.php> (November 20, 2005).

4. "21 questions with Tim Duncan," *Slamduncan.com,* November 2004, <http://www.slamduncan.com/news-21questions.php> (November 20, 2005).

5. S.L. Price, "The Quiet Man," *SI.com,* December 15, 2003, <http://pre-mium.si.cnn.com/pr/subs/siexclusive/2003/12/08/duncan1215/index.html> (November 14, 2005).

6. Ibid.

7. "Out of action," *CNNSI.com,* April 21, 2000, <http://sportsillustrated.cnn.com/basketball/nba/2000/playoffs/news/20 00/04/21/duncan_out_ap/> (December 9, 2005).

CHAPTER 9. SORROW AND JOY

1. Bob Hughes, "Duncan present in body, but in mind?," *ESPN.com*, May 3, 2001, <http://espn.go.com/nba/playoffs2002/columns/hughes_frank/2002/0503/1377427.html> (December 8, 2005).

2. Ibid.

3. "Spurs' Spark," *CNNSI.com*, May 4, 2002, <http://sportsillustrated.cnn.com/basketball/nba/2002/playoffs/news/2002/05/03/sonics_spurs_ap/> (December 8, 2005).

4. Ibid.

5. "Duncan wins first MVP; Kidd second, Shaq third," *ESPN.com*, May 9, 2002, <http://espn.go.com/nba/playoffs2002/s/2002/0509/1380580.html> (December 8, 2005).

CHAPTER 10. OLYMPIC DISAPPOINTMENT LEADS TO CHAMPIONSHIP CELEBRATION

1. Johnny Ludden, "The West is won: Duncan leads Spurs into Finals," *MySA.com*, June 2, 2005, <http://www.mysanantonio.com/sports/basketball/nba/spurs/stories/MYSA060205.1S.BKNspurs.suns.gamer5.2d25ee70b.html> (December 12, 2005).

2. James Brown, "Life is good in David Robinson's neighborhood," *SportingNews.com*, July 4, 2005, <http://www.sportingnews.com/exclusives/20050704/629652.html> (December 12, 2005).

3. "Spurs Dethrone Pistons To Take Third NBA Title," *NBA.com*, June 23, 2005, <http://aol.nba.com/games/20050623/DETSAS/recap.html> (December 11, 2005).

4. Ibid.

5. Johnny Ludden, "Spurs grind past Pistons to grab third NBA title," *MySA.com*, June 24, 2005, <http://www.mysanantonio.com/sports/basketball/nba/spurs/stories/MYSA062405.1S.BKNspurs.pistons.gamer7.f9cdbc.html> (December 12, 2005).

6. "Iverson and Duncan named USA co-captains," *InsideHoops.com*, July 27, 2004, <http://insidehoops.com/usa-072704.shtml> (December 10, 2005).

7. Chris Jenkins, "No sugar coating on bronze," *Signonsandiego.com*, August 29, 2004, <http://www.signonsandiego.com/sports/olympics/basketball/20040829-999-lz1x29sugar.html> (December 12, 2005).

8. Ibid.

9. Dave Glenn, "ACC in the NBA: Tim Duncan," *ACC Area Sports Journal*, May 5, 2003, <http://accsports.com/coverstory/xxvi/coverstoryxxvil8.jsp> (November 9, 2005).

GLOSSARY

assist—A pass that immediately precedes and sets up a scored basket.

backboard—The rectangular or fan-shaped board behind the basket.

bank shot—A shot where the ball is first bounced (or banked) off the backboard at such an angle that it then drops into the basket.

blocked shot—The successful deflection of a shot by touching part of the ball on its way to the basket, thereby preventing a field goal.

blocking out—A player's attempt to position his body between his opponent and the basket to get rebounds and prevent the opponents from doing so.

court vision—A player's ability to see everything on the court during play—such as where his teammates and defenders are set up—which enables him to make better choices in passing.

double-double—When a player scores double-digits in two categories during one game (points, assists, and rebounds are most common, but it can also be blocks or steals).

drive—A quick dribble directly to the basket in an effort to score.

dunk—When a player close to the basket jumps and strongly throws the ball down into it; an athletic, creative shot used to intimidate opponents.

free throw—An unguarded shot taken from behind the free-throw line after a foul. If successful, the shot counts as one point.

layup—A shot taken close to the basket that is usually banked off the backboard toward the basket.

paint—Also called the "key," "free-throw lane," or "lane," the free-throw line to the end line.

post—An offensive position played close to the basket along the key.

shooting range—The distance from which a player is likely to make his shots.

square up—When a player positions his shoulders to face the basket as he releases the ball for a shot; considered good shooting position.

three-pointer—A basket made from a distance greater than nineteen feet and nine inches during a high school or college game or twenty-three feet nine inches during a professional game.

triple-double—When a player scores double-digits in three categories during one game (points, assists, and rebounds are most common, but it can also be blocks or steals).

FOR MORE INFORMATION

FURTHER READING

Adams, Sean. *Sports Heroes and Legends – Tim Duncan.* Minneapolis, Minn.: Lerner Sports, 2004.

Byman, Jeremy. *Great Athletes: Tim Duncan.* Greensboro, N.C.: Morgan Reynolds, 2000.

Kernan, Kevin. *Tim Duncan: Slam Duncan.* Champaign, Ill: Sports Publishing, 2000.

WEB LINKS

Tim Duncan's Web page
Slamduncan.com

The Spurs' official Web site
Spurs.com

Web site devoted to the Spurs
Spursreport.com

Tim Duncan's page on NBA.com
NBA.com/playerfile/tim_duncan/

ESPN's official Web site
ESPN.com

INDEX

Duncan, Tim
    Associated Press Player of the Year, 44
    chooses basketball, 24
    debut with Spurs, 50–51
    growing up, 13, 15–20
    Home Team Community Service Award winner, 81
    MVP, 10–11, 13, 14, 20, 65, 70, 71, 81, 84, 95, 97, 102
    Naismith Award winner, 44
    Rookie of the Year, 57, 60, 74, 75, 89
    at St. Dunstan's Episcopal High School, 24, 26
    as swimmer, 15, 17–18, 20–21, 23–24, 43
    at Wake Forest, 32–38, 40–44, 45
    Wooden Award winner, 44
Duncan, Tricia, 16–17, 24, 27, 106
Duncan, William, 16, 22, 23, 27, 87, 88–89, 90–91, 92, 97, 106

E

Elie, Mario, 66
Elliott, Sean, 52, 70, 71, 83

G

Ginobili, Manu, 103, 111
Gundy, Jeff Van, 69, 111

R

Robinson, David, 6, 8, 9, 10, 14, 49, 51, 52, 53–54, 56–57, 59, 61, 63, 65, 67, 69, 72, 84, 86, 91, 97, 98, 102

Rogers, Rodney, 7

Russell, Bill, 10

S

San Antonio Spurs
   drafting Tim Duncan, 46, 48–49, 52

Seattle SuperSonics, 90, 91, 99

Sherrill, Amy, 14, 43, 75, 76, 77, 81–82, 99

Slam Duncans, 73

Smith, Charles, 52

Sprewell, Latrell, 63, 65–66

T

Tim Duncan Foundation, 13–14, 75–77, 81, 88

Tim Duncan's Character Program, 14, 77–79

U

Utah Jazz, 61, 70, 72, 95

V

Vancouver Grizzlies, 46, 94

Virgin Islands, 13, 14, 15, 18, 21, 22, 24, 26, 27, 30, 76, 77, 108